ROUTLEDGE LIBRARY EDITIONS: MANAGEMENT

Volume 29

MANAGING FOR PROFIT

MANAGING FOR PROFIT
The Added Value Concept

R. R. GILCHRIST

Routledge
Taylor & Francis Group

LONDON AND NEW YORK

First published in 1971 by George Allen & Unwin Ltd

This edition first published in 2018
by Routledge
2 Park Square, Milton Park, Abingdon, Oxon OX14 4RN

and by Routledge
711 Third Avenue, New York, NY 10017

Routledge is an imprint of the Taylor & Francis Group, an informa business

© 1971 George Allen & Unwin Ltd

British Library Cataloguing in Publication Data
A catalogue record for this book is available from the British Library

ISBN: 978-1-138-55938-7 (Set)
ISBN: 978-1-351-05538-3 (Set) (ebk)
ISBN: 978-1-138-56636-1 (Volume 29) (hbk)
ISBN: 978-1-315-12362-2 (Volume 29) (ebk)

Publisher's Note
The publisher has gone to great lengths to ensure the quality of this reprint but points out that some imperfections in the original copies may be apparent.

Disclaimer
The publisher has made every effort to trace copyright holders and would welcome correspondence from those they have been unable to trace.

MANAGING FOR PROFIT

The Added Value Concept

R. R. GILCHRIST

London
GEORGE ALLEN AND UNWIN LTD
RUSKIN HOUSE MUSEUM STREET

FIRST PUBLISHED IN 1971

© *George Allen & Unwin Ltd*, 1971

ISBN 0 04 658039 5

Printed in Great Britain
by The Aldine Press, Letchworth
in 11pt Times Roman

Preface

The origins of this book can be traced back to 1955. In that year, Peter Drucker's book, *The Practice of Management*, was published, and in it Drucker suggested that a productivity measure provides the only yardstick that can actually gauge the competence of management. Starting from Drucker's comments, the author decided to develop and test a productivity system based on Added Value as the measure of company income and output. The theory behind the system is that the behaviour of a company can best be explained in terms of its need to create an income. From this, it follows that its effectiveness depends on the efficiency with which it uses all the resources at its disposal to create this income. If it is accepted that the need is to create an income, then the efforts of the employees, the objectives of individuals, the pricing procedures, and the control systems must be co-ordinated to achieve this end. This is the underlying philosophy of the Added Value concept.

The author is not a professional economist, nor is he a professional accountant. He is a professional manager, who has written the book in terms that he himself can understand, in the knowledge that this will ensure that other professional managers will also be able to understand it. All the procedures described in the book have been used by operating companies, mainly in the Engineering Industry. Indeed, without such practical experience this book would not have been written, since little value can be attributed to theories untested in practice. It is hoped that the ideas propounded will be of assistance to managers grappling with the formidable problems of controlling companies in the complex industrial world of the 1970s.

R. GILCHRIST.

Contents

Chapter 1

The Nature of Company Income

The purpose of industry is the fulfilment of human needs. If industry can find customers for its products, sell these products at a profit, and operate within the limitations set by its social obligations, then it can justly claim that these needs are being satisfied.

No company can long survive without profit. Profit is the ultimate measure of effectiveness. A profitable company is likely to offer not only security of employment, but also promotion prospects, job opportunities, and the intense personal motivation that comes from being associated with success.

Mankind is insatiable in its desire for material possessions, as is industry in its search for markets. It is industry that makes and sells the consumer goods so coveted by the public, and it is the incomes generated within society that provide the means of purchase. If industry is efficient, goods will be freely available, at prices acceptable to the consumer. People will enjoy the high standard of living that is the direct result of high productivity. If industry is inefficient, then goods will be in short supply, prices will be high, and people will be discontented.

In the industrial context, efficiency and productivity are virtually synonymous. Each relates to the output resulting from a given input, and the need for constant productivity improvement is both a challenge and an objective to everyone concerned with the prosperity of industry. Assuming a steady level of employment, the standard of living of a nation is a function of its labour productivity, and the relationship between productivity, incomes, and prices has been so well publicized in recent years that few people are entirely ignorant of it.

We have already said that the purpose of industry is the fulfilment of human needs, but it must be admitted that most people find it difficult to equate abstract definitions with the severely practical aspects of their daily tasks. Theory is all very well, but the duty of management is to achieve results, and one must be very clear about the nature of these results before one can measure progress towards them. Without doubt, the final result must be profit, and a business can only earn a profit if it is able to utilize its resources effectively, harness the skills and abilities of its employees, innovate, exploit new markets, and locate and develop new opportunities. It must know its strengths and weaknesses, where it is going, and how it is going to get there.

A business has many resources, each of which is an integral component of successful operation. For example, a manufacturing company has buildings, machines, tools, handling equipment, raw materials, stocks, and many other items which contribute towards the finished product. The essential basis of every cost reduction programme is that it should reduce the resource content of the finished product so that, for a given selling price, the profit content will increase. Here we have the real fundamental of company operation, namely, that a business has only a certain income available to it. If it allocates too much of this income to labour and the other items of cost, then too little will remain for profit. An unsatisfactory profit implies an unsatisfactory cash flow, and if this is inadequate the company will be unable to replace machines, purchase new equipment, or provide additional working capital for expansion.

As we shall see in later chapters, the true income of a company is obtained by deducting, from the value of sales, the value of all raw materials and other bought-out purchases. This income represents the fund from which all wages, salaries, and profits must be paid, as well as other items of operating expense, such as rent, rates, and depreciation. The name given to this fund is 'Added Value'.

Added Value* has long been used by national statisticians for measuring the income – and hence the output – of a country, but it is only comparatively recently that companies have become aware of the great potential inherent in the Added Value concept as a tool of management. A result of this has been the recognition that the creation of Added Value is a primary business objective. Companies such as Laporte Industries, Delta Metal, and High Duty Alloys have done much valuable work in the development of Added Value control ratios for

* Also called Value Added. In this book, the term 'Value Added' is used in the context of company taxation only.

performance appraisal – an area of particular relevance to holding companies, where the problem of controlling a number of diverse operating companies poses very real difficulties.

The creation of Added Value is an objective which ought constantly to be in the minds of company executives. Whenever decisions are taken, the acid test of their effectiveness will be whether they have resulted in an improvement in the Added Value per unit of resource input. Eventually, of course, greater effectiveness must result in increased profits, but this may take some time to happen. The reason for this is that profits are volume sensitive, that is, they are affected by changes in output. The lower the output, the higher the fixed costs per unit of output, and the lower the profit. Conversely, the higher the output, the higher the profit.

Every investor is aware of the fact that adverse trading conditions generally cause a decline in profits. Because of this it is not easy to assess the true profit potential of a company simply by looking at the published accounts for a given year. It is much more meaningful to analyse results covering several years, so that trends may be established, and conclusions inferred regarding the progress of the business. In the short term, it is not possible to judge the performance of a company on profits alone. Profits are the effects resulting from wise decisions; it is the causes relating to these decisions which the company analyst must endeavour to understand.

Business prosperity depends on many factors, all interwoven and difficult to disentangle. Some are subjective, consisting of intangibles such as company image, market standing, technical expertise, customer satisfaction and quality of product. Others are more factual, such as cost of production, raw material utilization, labour and capital productivity, and price levels. These are all measurable, and indeed must be measured if a company is to be controlled. There are examples of companies which operate on the intuition of the chief executive, but these are becoming much rarer as industrial life becomes ever more competitive. They are becoming rarer either because companies have found intuition to be unsatisfactory, or else because they have gone bankrupt.

By far the most difficult aspect of business administration is concerned with taking decisions, particularly in the subjective areas where opinions may differ, facts are in short supply, and action is necessary. A good management accounting system should enable senior executives to locate areas of developing inefficiency, whether these relate to people, to machines or to any other element of production cost. It is easy to know when things are going wrong. It is very difficult to know what should be done about it. This is where managerial expertise and flair are vitally necessary, for without these characteristics the best information system ever developed will be sterile and useless.

The universal sales and cost equation relating to a company trading at a profit is:

Value of Sales = Cost of external purchases+Labour Cost+Fixed Costs+Profit

The external purchases represent the value of everything the company has bought. They include raw materials, tools, consumable stores, electricity, gas, coal, fuel oil, acid, and other similar items used to convert goods from one form to another. In other words, if we deduct these variable costs from the value of sales, we obtain the Added Value. We can, therefore, rewrite the equation as follows:

Profit = Added Value—(Labour Cost+Fixed Costs)
= Net Income—Operating Expenses

The object of quoting this equation is simply to stress that Added Value is the net income of a company, after it has paid all its external suppliers. Once this is fully appreciated, it will be apparent why company control systems should be designed to focus attention on the relationship of operating costs to Added Value, rather than on the more customary relationship of costs to Sales Value.

To maximize Profit we need to maximize Added Value. This must be the objective, and all a company's policies should be directed to this end, provided always that it does not achieve the end at the expense of its social obligations.

During the nineteenth century economists became increasingly concerned about the possibility that private monopolies could control trade within a country, and Karl Marx believed that it was inevitable that more and more of a nation's wealth would be accumulated by fewer and fewer enterprises. Both these attitudes were largely conditioned by fear of the disproportionate power which could be wielded by those in charge of large concentrations of wealth.

In recent years there has been renewed concern regarding the dominance of large public companies. In America, the top 200 companies employ one eighth of the total U.S. labour force, and own just under one quarter of all industrial assets. The largest of them all, General Motors, has an annual sales turnover exceeding the national product of all but a few nations. The power wielded by the President of General Motors, and the effect his decisions can have on the well-being of many hundreds of thousands of employees, is awe-inspiring indeed.

Power is undoubtedly an extraordinarily strong motivating factor. Power and a sense of achievement are complementary. One is reminded of the leading industrialist who said, 'I love my job because of the power I wield. If the company stopped paying me, I think I would be prepared to carry on for nothing.' That this industrialist was exceptionally honest and hard working no one can deny. Yet society could well ask whether a similar man, with fewer scruples, would hesitate to act in a thoroughly anti-social, and even dishonest way, if this were the means of retaining his power.

The purpose of industry is the fulfilment of human needs. The source of this definition is paragraph 3 of the Marlow Declaration, signed in 1962 by a group of industrialists, trade union leaders, Church and Government representatives. These men considered that it was their duty to try to define the responsibilities of industry, in the hope that their creed would give guidance to others. Few people now remember the Marlow Declaration, which is unfortunate, as it was a sincere and honest attempt to define an industrial philosophy. It stated that industry has five responsibilities, namely to the employee, the shareholder, the consumer, the local community and the nation. These responsibilities were further amplified as follows:

To the employee: Fair wages, security, status, comradeship, scope for self development and self fulfilment. Good and safe working conditions. Pride in skill, and a sense of belonging. Value to others of work done.

To the shareholder: A fair and reasonable return on invested capital.

To the consumer: Good quality at a fair price.

To the local community: To be a good neighbour, taking a constructive interest in local affairs.

To the nation: The proper and productive use and development of resources, both human and material, for which it is responsible.

13

An enterprise, if it is to remain in business and generate employment, must make profits, and must constantly strive for ways and means of reducing costs. There is always a better way, and the search for this must be unending. Nevertheless, in a world where it is increasingly fashionable to question motives, no company can afford to remain indifferent to its social obligations, or to pursue profit with scant regard for human dignity. The belief that the end justifies the means is no longer acceptable in a free society, and the company that neglects public opinion in its business transactions does so at its peril.

Chapter 2

Men, Motivation and Money

It is generally assumed that the main reason why people go to work is for the money they earn. This is true in that no one would be prepared of his own free will to work for nothing – unless of course he had a private income, and there was some other factor, such as the enjoyment of power, which was all-important.

While it is almost certainly true that people go to work for the money they can earn, it would be untrue to assume that money is necessarily the most important factor leading to job satisfaction. Too often this is assumed to be the case, and as a result there has developed the widely accepted philosophy that, by offering the opportunity of monetary reward, people will behave exactly as required.

Between 1958 and 1963 the author had the opportunity of talking to several hundred supervisors, in groups of about twenty, in the Wolverhampton, Birmingham and Coventry areas. During these talks the supervisors were asked to fill in a questionnaire, so as to find out what they thought were the matters of greater or lesser importance to work-people on the shop floor.

Before the forms were completed, it was stressed that the supervisors should put themselves in the place of the shop floor personnel they supervised. The object was to find out what the supervisors *thought* were the attitudes of those they supervised, and not what the supervisors thought themselves.

The supervisors were given a form which listed eight factors which the shop floor employees were likely to consider as having some relevance to their jobs. To illustrate the thinking behind the questionnaire, the case of two factories, A and B, operating in the same town and in the same street, was first considered. Factory A pays 10 per cent more

15

money per hour than B. If both are short of labour, why do not all the employees at B queue up for jobs at A? If they do not do so, presumably there are a number of other factors concerning their jobs at factory B which are considered important. It was to ascertain the supervisors' views on this that the survey was conducted.

The list of elements of job satisfaction comprised eight items as follows:

ELEMENTS OF JOB IMPORTANCE

Element

1. Prospects of promotion.
2. Good wages.
3. Good working conditions.
4. Sympathetic and helpful treatment with personal problems.
5. Tactful disciplining.
6. Job security.
7. Being kept informed on Company affairs.
8. Working on interesting jobs.

At the start of this research project it was not known how the supervisors would vote. After only three groups had completed the questionnaire it became very obvious that a distinct pattern was emerging, and that it should be possible to predict with fair accuracy the way the next group of supervisors would vote. This prediction was made at each ensuing session, being circulated while the results of the survey were being analysed. A composite table is given below showing (a) the order of importance in which supervisors thought shop floor employees would rank the factors, (b) the prediction made as a result of previous polls, and (c) the way in which an actual sample of shop floor employees recorded their votes.

Element		*Priority*	
	a	*b*	*c*
1. Prospects for promotion	4	3	6
2. Good wages	1	1	4
3. Good working conditions	3	4	7
4. Sympathetic and helpful treatment with personal problems	8	8	2
5. Tactful disciplining	7	7	8
6. Job security	2	2	1
7. Being kept informed on Company affairs	6	6	3
8. Working on interesting jobs	5	5	5

16

Rather than look at the results of this survey in numerical sequence, it is probably better to list the eight items in two groups of four. The first group we will label 'more important', the second 'less important'. Listing the shop floor order of preference as given above we have:

More Important
   Job security   S
   Help with personal problems
   Being kept informed on Company affairs
   Good wages   S

Less Important
   Working on interesting jobs
   Prospects for promotion   S
   Good working conditions   S
   Tactful disciplining

The items marked S are those which the supervisors thought 'more important'. Not just one particular group, but every single group participating in the survey overlooked the two items of *'Being kept informed on Company affairs'* and *'Help with personal problems'* as having much significance. This is particularly interesting.

As a follow-up to the survey, a number of supervisors were interviewed, and asked a series of questions regarding their present and past occupations. One particular question was, 'Who was the best boss you have ever worked for?' Having given the answer, the next question was, 'Can you give any specific reasons for your choice?' In the majority of cases, one of the reasons given was that the best boss was interested in his subordinates. He had confidence in them, and he took them into his confidence. In one case mentioned, the boss even made a point of visiting his subordinates when they were ill. Was this not an example of help with personal problems?

We must beware lest we draw false conclusions from a simple survey such as the one described. Obviously, if a company is paying wages well below the average, the labour force is likely to consider money of primary importance. Similarly, if a company has a deplorable safety record, good working conditions are likely to be of considerable significance. It is not proposed to discuss this particular survey further. The results are not really surprising to students of motivation, and merely confirm the findings of many more extensive polls. It does, however, underline the fallacy of the common assumption that money

17

is the most important factor in a job. A common assumption, but far from true.

So far in this chapter we have discussed motivation, and have mentioned the word money. What then is money? How much money should be paid for a given job? How much of its income can a company distribute to its employees? Do high wages cause unemployment? All these questions are of extreme relevance to the manager of today, girt around as he is with restrictions, claims for higher wages, exhortations to match wages with productivity, and so on. Even to argue forcefully and effectively, the manager of the 1970s must be part-economist, or else he will be unable to explain the basic problems affecting every company in a nation reliant on international trade for a satisfactory standard of living.

What is money? This sounds a very stupid question. Money is what you use to buy things: money is – well – money. More often than not, there the definition ends. At a recent management development course for senior managers, held at the training establishment of one of Britain's largest industrial concerns, not one of the syndicate members was able to define money. Yet these very men were all likely to return to their respective firms at the end of the course, and be involved, within a matter of hours, in money problems.

The word 'pecuniary' gives a clue to the origins of money. The origin of pecuniary lies in the word '*pecu*', meaning livestock, or cattle in particular. The Latin '*pecunia*' and the old European word '*fihu*', from whence feudal and fee, also related to cattle. In the early days of civilization, a man's wealth was measured by the number of his cattle and other livestock. This was particularly the case with the Zulus, where the royal herds represented the wealth of the nation, and exceptional service was rewarded with the gift of cows. Cows were the marriage dowry. Cows were money.

Money has several important attributes. It must be easily recognized and easily transferable. It must be limited in supply. Preferably it should have high value and small bulk. Cows qualify under the first three headings, possibly the fourth and certainly not the fifth. Besides, no one would, under normal circumstances, accept payment for goods in cows. Cigarettes, yes: cows, no.

The economists' definition of money is that it is a means of exchange and a measure of value. It is also a store of value. People using money

18

as a means of exchange, that is, in payment for goods and services rendered, must have confidence in the value it represents. Without confidence in its value, money can no longer be a means of exchange, and thus ceases to be money. A Republic of Ireland ten penny piece is the same size and weight as an English ten penny piece, and superficially looks the same. Many Irish ten penny pieces have been used as money in England, but only because the recipients have not noticed what they were accepting. Had they noticed, they would undoubtedly have refused them in payment of a transaction. Why? Because the recipient would have lacked confidence that someone else, in their turn, would have accepted the Irish coin in payment for goods or services rendered. Thus the Irish coin, though money in Ireland, is not money in England.

Money is a Means of Exchange
Life in all but the most primitive societies would cease to exist as we know it if there were no means of exchange other than barter. The division of labour – that is, job specialization – would be an impossibility, and about the only people who would manage to survive in a total-barter society would be those who were able to grow sufficient food to keep themselves alive. The rest would perish without ever finding a person who would exchange the means of existence for the results of their labour.

Industry, commerce, and modern society can only survive because money provides the means of exchange. If money is scarce, then the economic tempo is reduced, incomes are affected and hence expenditure reduced. If expenditure is reduced, then the sure and certain result is that unemployment will rise.

In the early days of the twentieth century it used to be considered that the state, which can make money, must under no circumstances issue money which could not be backed by gold. If it were to do so, then inflation would result. The disastrous behaviour of the German mark immediately after the first world war gave support to these ideas, and it was not until the Gold Standard was finally abolished in the early 1930s that realization slowly dawned regarding the true causes of inflation.

In Britain, during the bleak and terrible days of depression before the second world war, the coal miners of Wales would gladly have dug coal to warm the cold and despondent farmers of Norfolk if only they could have exchanged their coal for food. Similarly, the farmers of

19

Norfolk would have been eager and willing to grow food for the hungry miners of Wales, if only they could have had some coal in return. Sadly there was no opportunity for barter, and there was no means of exchange. Why then did not the Government print money? Because it was afraid of inflation, and because it only imperfectly understood monetary theory.

In fact, of course, inflation results when too much money is available to purchase too few goods. This is called demand inflation, and occurs when resources are fully utilized, or virtually fully utilized. Under such circumstances more purchasing power causes prices to rise as demand exceeds supply. If, however, resources are far from fully utilized, as was the case in the depression of the 1930s, more purchasing power simply results in more resources being put to work, more goods being produced, and more employment being generated. In the depression years inflation would not have resulted until demand exceeded supply, or unless costs ran riot, both unlikely contingencies with a high level of unemployment. The creation of money as a means of exchange would have been well justified. Unfortunately old-fashioned theories prevailed to the detriment of millions of people.

Money is a Measure of Value
Every schoolboy knows that one cannot add up the value of five apples, four oranges and three pears without expressing each in a common term, namely money. Similarly, the factors of production represented in a company balance sheet must be reduced to the common denominator of money before one can assess the relative value of land, buildings, machines, stocks and so on.

An eminent industrialist once regretted that the employees were not valued in monetary terms and included in the balance sheet. In his opinion, were this to be done, the directors and shareholders might form a better judgment of the true value of the employees; at the least, the very action of valuing executives, managers, supervisors, and others for inclusion in the balance sheet would be salutary.

Money is a Store of Value
The royal herds of the Zulu kings were the national store of wealth. The king regarded himself as the custodian of this wealth, holding it in trust against the lean years when it would be needed.

Money is only a store of value as long as its purchasing power does not alter. This was well appreciated in Tudor days, when Gresham expounded his famous law that bad money drives out good. Consider what would happen if a country which uses eighteen-carat gold coins decides to reduce the gold content, and issue nine-carat coins. The result would be that the eighteen-carat coins would tend to disappear from circulation. People would realize immediately that the eighteen-carat coins were a better store of value – safer from the effects of inflation – than nine-carat. Consequently, a person would hoard all the eighteen-carat coins coming into his possession, exchanging only coins with a lower gold content in return for goods and services.

The early economists, including the renowned John Stuart Mill, were of the opinion that the value of money did not really matter. Double all wages, they said, and you would double all prices. One pound sterling would then be worth only fifty pence, but there would be no alteration in the goods and services provided. A fifty pence saucepan would therefore cost one hundred pence, but since incomes had doubled, nobody would be any better or any worse off.

For wage and salary earners there is a certain amount of truth in this statement. However, it must be appreciated that a considerable proportion of the population, such as pensioners, have to exist on a fixed salary. Further, there is the problem of long term debt under conditions of rising prices. The higher the prices, the easier it is to pay debts, since the interest on loans is generally at a given rate on a stated sum. The principal does not change as a result of price inflation, but its purchasing power does.

The most serious end result of reducing the value of money within a country would undoubtedly be to weaken its competitive ability as an international trader. As long as unit labour costs within a country are rising at about the same rate as those of its major trading competitors, then it should remain competitive. If, on the other hand, labour costs rise more steeply, it is only a matter of time before markets are lost, and exports slump. Devaluation may restore the situation as a once off measure. The long term answer must be to do all possible to stabilize prices, both by controlling and by preventing earnings rising faster than labour productivity.

Whether stabilized prices can ever be achieved in a democratic society without a high rate of unemployment is a matter for conjecture.

21

Certainly, there is little evidence of stability if one examines the published statistics of the main industrial nations.

Money is a means of exchange, a measure of value and a store of value. Money can be made by the state, in the form of bonds, bills and currency. Money can be made by an individual, if he is sufficiently skilled as a forger to be able to produce a product which is accepted as a means of exchange.

Swindlers and forgers apart, money can be made by the state and money can be created by banks. Many people falsely believe that banks are only able to lend by advancing money which has previously been loaned to them. In other words, if Smith pays £50 cash into his bank, he converts the £50 cash into a £50 claim on the bank. The banking system relies on the fact that all the Smiths in the country are unlikely to demand repayment of their individual £50 cash credits at one and the same time. Accordingly, after prudently setting aside part of the deposit to maintain an acceptable cash : deposits ratio, the bank then lends the balance – say £45 – to worthy borrowers. To a banker, of course, the definition 'worthy' as applied to a borrower means that he doesn't really need the money, and is able to repay it at a minute's notice. This lending against bank deposits is a perfectly normal and acceptable way of providing finance, but it does not involve banks in the manufacture of money.

Banks make money by creating credit. They create the means of payment out of nothing.

This statement is, to many people, so bordering on heresy that it is worth repeating. *Banks make money by creating credit. They create the means of payment out of nothing.* It may seem impossible, but a moment's reflection will make it plain that this is exactly what banks can, and frequently do, do. Consider a small business, expanding vigorously, and with a product generally accepted to be a market leader. Rapid expansion is always a time for close financial scrutiny, as there is a real danger of running out of money, because wages and salaries are the first claims on company assets. Also customers have the tiresome characteristic of demanding at least ten weeks' credit when the conditions of sale plainly state 'net monthly account'.

The first thing any small business does when it shows signs of running out of money – assuming that it has recognized the signs, which is not always the case – is to try to arrange a bank overdraft. If the bank is convinced that the loan is worth while, then what happens? The bank makes money by creating a credit against which the business has the right to draw. The bank has made money where there was none before. It has, perhaps even more convincingly than the magician who produces a rabbit out of a hat, done the seemingly impossible. With a stroke of a pen, it has made money.

Money, then, can be made by the state, and created by banks. Whoever it was that invented money (and it was probably a Babylonian) could well reflect that his invention has had a greater effect on the welfare of mankind than any other.

An understanding of the essential features and characteristics of money is very necessary in the industrial field. It is not necessary that one should be able to debate the finer points of monetary theory with a professional economist. It is necessary that one should be able to define money, and to appreciate its relevance in today's world.

Chapter 3

Incomes and Employment

To the ancient Greeks, economics was the art of managing the household resources. That was the original meaning of the word, although like so many others its emphasis has changed with the passing of the years. Nowadays when we refer to economics, we are speaking of the management of the nation's resources, and the effect such management has on society. Economics is concerned with the provision of services, with taxation, with investment and with the creation of wealth.

Although economics is concerned with the creation of wealth, it is perhaps worth recording that, while the alternative ways and means of producing wealth are very much the province of the economist, what one does with the wealth created is the province of the politician. Economists certainly will try to state the possible effects of distributing wealth in this way or that, even though their views tend to depend on the theory that is in vogue at a particular moment of time. The actual decisions regarding what will be done are taken by politicians.

Irrespective of which political party is in power, there is general agreement that the primary objective of economic policy is to secure the maximum good for the largest possible number of people. An obvious way of doing this is to increase the national income – assuming of course that any increase achieved is fairly distributed over the whole community.

The standard of living of a community can be expressed as the national income per head. If the national income in the United Kingdom were thirty-three thousand million pounds, and there were fifty-five million people living in the country, then the national income per head would be £600. This £600 per head would thus become a measure of the nation's prosperity. To many people, their standard of living means the

24

number of motor cars they possess, the television sets, the size of house, the deep freezes, and all the other material things of life. In fact, as is readily apparent from a real understanding of the distribution of national income, a nation could have a very high standard of living without having many material things to show for it. For example, supposing the half-million persons employed in the United Kingdom motor vehicle industry suddenly stopped making cars and motor components, and began building tanks and armoured cars. Suppose further that the nation decided to spend its income not by purchasing motor cars, which are dangerous sources of atmospheric pollution, but by supporting the arts, theatre, ballet, opera, and so on. The money previously spent on motor cars would be spent on the arts. The nation would have the finest ballet, and the army would have the best equipped armoured divisions in the world. The national income per head would remain unchanged, yet few people would own a motor car.

Consumer goods are the outward and visible signs of a society with a high standard of living. Hence the general confusion about the meaning of the phrase, and its association with purely material things. National prosperity is a function of the national income. Half the national income could be removed by taxation, under a ruthless Government unconcerned with such ephemeral matters as democratic elections, and spent on wise or foolish projects such as space rockets, hospitals, schools, the arts, welfare, and maintaining a powerful standing army. The population as a whole, after tax, might be very poor, and hardly able to afford such necessities of life as two motor cars, a television set in every room, and a holiday in Majorca each spring and autumn. Yet their standard of living, in terms of national income per head, could be very high indeed.

In any discussion concerning national income or national productivity, where the pound sterling is used as a measure of value and of output, care must be taken to ensure that suitable allowance is made to compensate for any changes which may have occurred in the value of money over time.

Suppose that, over five years, the monetary value of all incomes rose by 40 per cent. If one knew that the population had remained absolutely static, one might be tempted to infer that the real income per head of population had also risen by 40 per cent. Before one could say this, the changes in price levels over the period would have to be

25

examined. Almost certainly, as everyone is aware, particularly those living on fixed incomes, prices would have risen, say by 20 per cent over the five years. The pound, which had a purchasing power of one hundred pence five years ago, would thus have a purchasing power of some eighty-three pence as a result of the price increases. Further, the average income per head would only have risen by 16⅔ per cent in real terms, as against the apparent 40 per cent before adjustment was made for price changes.

We have seen in Chapter 2 that money is a means of exchange, a measure of value, and a store of value. What then can one say about incomes, in order to define their place in the economy?

The output of the economy, both goods and services, can be measured in three different ways. By adding up all incomes, by adding up all expenditure, and by adding up the value of all output. Whichever way is used, the answer should be the same, but a moment's reflection will reveal the enormous difficulties inherent in gathering the relevant statistics in an advanced economy. Consequently, the three methods do tend to give three different results, although these are generally not too far apart to invalidate comparisons.

To understand the relationship between incomes, expenditure and output it is necessary to consider the circulation of money within an economy. Two years before the battle of Trafalgar, the great French economist, J. B. Say, held the cheerful view that the productive capacity of a nation would always be fully utilized. Supply created its own demand, and hence overproduction was impossible. Admittedly, Say realized very well that overproduction might occur in certain areas of the economy, where people had sufficient of the product being manu-factured. However, he considered that, since man was acquisitive and would always buy goods to the limits of his income, this localized overproduction, and the unemployment which it would cause, was merely temporary, and would last only until labour could be transferred to make those goods which were still in demand.

The key feature in Say's theory was the assumption that people would always buy goods to the limits of their incomes. This can best be appreciated by a diagrammatic representation of the primary circula-tion of goods and services within the economy, as in Figure 1.

Figure 1 shows the economy, consisting of households and firms. The households provide the factors of production, in the form of land, capital and labour, to the firms. In return, the firms provide the households with incomes. The households then spend these incomes on goods and services which are provided by the firms. The circulation flow is now complete. In Figure 1, Y represents the incomes paid in return for the factors of production provided by the households. Having received the income Y, the households then proceed to spend it by purchasing goods and services Cg, the money that they pay to the firms for these goods and services being Cx, the consumption expenditure.

FIGURE 1

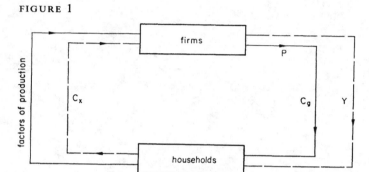

It will be readily apparent that the production of goods and services (P) is equal to the consumption of goods and services (Cg). Also the national income Y is equal to the expenditure on goods and services (Cx).

Thus:

$$P = Cg \qquad \text{(i)}$$
$$Y = Cx \qquad \text{(ii)}$$

But $\qquad P = Y$

$\therefore \qquad Cg = Cx \qquad \text{(iii)}$

Figure 1 indicates the underlying argument behind Say's theory. The more the productive capacity available in the firms, the more the employment, and the more the incomes; the more the incomes, the more the money that will be spent on goods and services. This figure also illustrates two important principles:

1. The value of all incomes equals the value of all output;
2. Every penny of every price is somebody's income.

If people spent every penny they earned, and the circulation of goods and incomes was as simple as in Figure 1, then undoubtedly the produc-

27

tive capacity of the nation would always be fully utilized, and the firms would have no difficulty in selling their products. The one great and conclusive argument against this assumption is that people do not spend every penny of their income. Even if they think they do, because their expenditure exactly equals their income, a proportion of their expenditure is always almost certainly spent on items such as insurance and pension premiums, both of which represent a form of saving.

To examine a slightly more sophisticated model of the economy, we must look at Figure 2.

FIGURE 2

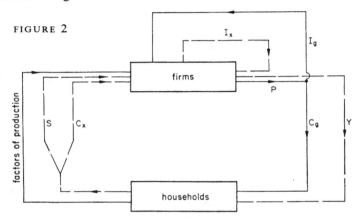

In Figure 2, the households provide the factors of production, and obtain incomes in return. Not all the incomes are spent on consumer goods, however. A proportion (Cx) is used to buy goods (Cg), but the remainder of the incomes are set aside in savings, which find their way back to the firms, and can be used for investment purposes. The firms also generate savings out of their retained profits, and these too go back to the firms for investment.

Referring to Figure 2, the national production P consists of Consumption goods and Investment goods. The national income Y is either spent on consumption (Cx) or saved (S).

Thus we have:

$$P = Cg + Ig \qquad \text{(i)}$$
$$Y = Cx + S \qquad \text{(ii)}$$
Now $\quad Cg = Cx$
$\therefore \qquad Ig = S \qquad \text{(iii)}$

From Figure 2 we begin to obtain an appreciation of the relationship between savings and investment. In the early days of the nineteenth century economists were aware of this relationship, but they considered that investments were the result of savings. It was John Maynard Keynes, whose great work *The General Theory of Employment, Interest and Money* did so much to demolish the classical views of economic theory between the wars, who argued that savings were the result of investment – the exact opposite of the classical theory.

It is doubtful whether any economist would be prepared to risk his reputation by trying to prove whether savings are the cause, or the effect, of investment. Suffice it to say that the equality of savings and investment is an extremely important feature of economic theory. As incomes increase, history indicates that savings, as a percentage of incomes, also increase. Thus investment increases. As investment increases, so does productivity – assuming always that the investment has been made wisely. As productivity increases, so does the national income per head, with consequent benefits to all in a higher standard of living.

A feature of democratic societies which causes much grief to those who wish to forecast, plan, execute and control is that people, when allowed to do so, tend to make decisions which, although insignificant individually, collectively upset the ideas of the all-wise and all-powerful who seek to determine the course of human events. If the all-wise and all-powerful could only predict, with reasonable accuracy, the savings of the nation, then they could also predict the consumption and the investment.

One of the main foundations of the dogma, popular in some circles, that wealth should be more evenly distributed across the population, is that the propensity to save of the very rich is less easy to predict than of the less well-off. One might well counter this by suggesting that a much better control of the economy could be achieved by encouraging a small number of people to accumulate vast wealth. Having obligingly done so, one could then instruct these very rich people to spend, if the economy required it, or, in other circumstances, instruct them to save. Failure to comply would result in swingeing taxation, and the very rich would thus have no acceptable alternative to doing what they were told. If the economy needed a boost, they would buy new Rolls-Royce motor cars, gold plated Daimlers, or throw extravagant parties in

Mayfair. If the economy was over-heating, they would save busily, withdrawing purchasing power and reducing demand – inflationary pressures. Every manager of any competence realizes that he must concentrate on those few facets of his job which contribute most towards the objective. It is always easier to control the few than to influence the many. Is there then not a good economic case for encouraging the few to achieve great wealth, and influencing them in their patterns of saving and expenditure? Economically this might be very sound but it would hardly be in accordance with the mood of the times!

In times of full employment, saving reduces demand, and hence assists exports and the control of prices. In times of unemployment, spending increases demand, and generates employment. The generation of employment by spending was quickly appreciated by Hitler in the 1930s, with the result that Nazi Germany soon became the most powerful nation in Europe, with a high national income and low unemployment.

To appreciate the employment which is generated by spending, let us suppose that the Government decides to proceed with the construction of a Channel tunnel, requiring a total of 5,000 workers for the enterprise. The average weekly wage is £40, and we will examine the total expenditure resulting from one week's income assuming:

Situation (a) Saving at the rate of 10 per cent for all receiving an income, directly or indirectly, from the tunnel enterprise.

Or

Situation (b) Saving at the rate of 20 per cent for all receiving an income.

The formula for the summation of a series, of which the first term is A, each successive term being $r \times$ the preceding term, is:

$$\text{Sum of terms} = A \times \frac{1}{1-r}$$

Table 1 indicates the saving and total expenditure relating to the two assumptions in (a) and (b) above. To interpret this table it has to be appreciated that the 5,000 workers on the tunnel receive £200,000 per week for their labour. They spend £180,000 of this in the first situation (a), and save £20,000. The £180,000 then becomes an income for other people, say shopkeepers and publicans, who in their turn spend £162,000 and save £18,000, or 10 per cent, and so on to the end of the incomes chain. The situation (*b*) is similar, excepting that 80 per cent of the incomes are spent and 20 per cent saved.

TABLE 1: CHANNEL TUNNEL PROJECT

Situation (a)		Situation (b)	
Incomes = £200,000		Incomes = £200,000	
Expenditure £	*Saving* @ 10% £	*Expenditure* £	*Saving* @ 20% £
180,000	20,000	160,000	40,000
162,000	18,000	128,000	32,000
145,800	16,200	102,400	25,600
etc.	etc.	etc.	etc.
Total £1,800,000	£200,000	£800,000	£200,000

In case (*a*) the total expenditure contributing to employment is £1,800,000 plus the initial £200,000, or £2,000,000. In case (*b*) the total is £1,000,000. Since the employment generated is a function of total expenditure, and total expenditure equals total incomes, it is readily evident that case (*a*) generates twice the employment of case (*b*). Further, and perhaps surprisingly, the total amount saved in each case is £200,000 – exactly the same as the initial wage and salary bill!

This simple example is an illustration of the relationship between the level of savings and the generation of employment. In times of boom, when unemployment is less than, say, $1\frac{1}{2}$ per cent, increasing the rate of saving will reduce overall expenditure and hence the demand for labour. It should also diminish the risk of prices rising due to excessive demand.

In times of slump, when unemployment is higher than, say $2\frac{1}{2}$ per cent (shades of Beveridge, who defined full employment at a level of 3 per cent unemployed) a reduction in the rate of saving will increase the overall expenditure, and in so doing create employment.

So far we have examined a very simple model of the circulation of money in the economy, and a slightly more complex model incorporating savings and investment. To complete the review, it is now necessary to look at the flow in a system which includes provision for taxation,

31

Government expenditure, and foreign trade. This is illustrated in Figure 3.

In contrast to Figures 1 and 2, where the circulation was between households and firms, we now have a third factor to consider, namely the Government. Further, instead of a closed domestic economy, where employment is unlikely to be affected by changes in wage rates, we have an international economy, with the households purchasing imported goods (if they are more competitive than the home-produced articles) and the firms selling goods for export (if they are more competitive than foreign articles).

FIGURE 3

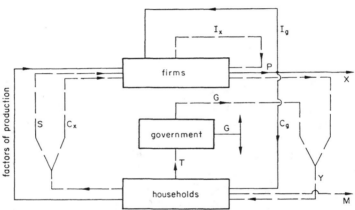

Analysis of Figure 3 shows that the production of goods and services (P) divides into three streams, namely consumption goods and services (Cg), investment (Ig) and Exports (X). In addition, the Government also produces a certain amount of goods and services which are distributed either to the firms or to the households.

The national income is allocated to consumption (Cx), saving (S), imports (M) or taxes (T).

We have therefore the following situation:

$$P = Cg + Ig + X + G \qquad \text{(i)}$$
$$Y = Cx + S + M + T \qquad \text{(ii)}$$

Now
$$P = Y \quad \text{and} \quad Cg = Cx$$

∴
$$Ig + X + G = S + M + T \qquad \text{(iii)}$$

32

Equation (iii) is indicative of the relationships which must exist if the economy is to remain in equilibrium. It has been said, quite rightly, that exporting goods results in exporting unemployment. In other words, every time a product is sold in the export market, employment has been generated at home, and a loss of employment opportunity generated in the purchasing country – assuming of course that it is able to produce this particular product.

Investment, exports, and Government expenditure are all inflationary, in that incomes are generated without any corresponding goods being produced for purchase. Savings, imports and taxation are deflationary. If exports rise, the national income will lose equilibrium, which can be regained by increasing savings, imports, or taxation. From the point of view of the impact on the economy, it does not matter at all which of the three is increased. From the point of view of the individual, it matters a great deal!

Figures 1, 2, and 3 illustrate progressively more complex situations affecting the flow of incomes and expenditure within the economy. The national income is determined by total expenditure, and this expenditure in turn determines levels of employment. An economy which does not rely on international trade for the prosperity of its people does not have to worry too much about increased wage rates affecting employment. The higher costs which result are virtually counterbalanced by the greater purchasing power provided, although, as has been mentioned previously, the resulting higher prices would cause hardship to those living on fixed incomes.

Few industrialized countries can claim that their prosperity is not affected by their level of exports. If a country is to be competitive in the export markets of the world, its wage costs per unit of output must also be competitive. To sell a product one must find a customer with sufficient purchasing power to pay the asking price; if the asking price is too high, owing to excessive costs or profits, there will be no sale.

A country whose unit wage costs are rising faster than those of its main competitors, because of an adverse trend in the relationship between wages and productivity, will be faced with the progressive loss of its export markets. To any country which is heavily dependent on its ability to export, such a loss could well lead to a progressive increase in levels of unemployment.

33

Chapter 4

Prosperity and Productivity

The productive capacity of a firm is built up as a result of the combination of a great number of diverse factors. It is the effectiveness of this combination which is the direct reflection of managerial ability. Good management will constantly endeavour to extract the maximum potential from people, from machines, from space and from all the resources committed to its charge. Bad management will underestimate the ability of people to achieve results (always assuming that the required results are clearly defined), and will fail to deploy resources efficiently, tending to find excuses for each and every setback encountered.

One is reminded of the attitude of Napoleon after a particular battle in which the French, for once, were not devastatingly successful. As was his practice, Napoleon subsequently discussed the battle tactics with his generals, to find out and if possible to learn from the mistakes which were made. One after another the generals made their excuses. The ground was softer than expected on the left flank. The bad visibility hampered the *francs-tireurs*. The British withstood successive charges by the Guard, instead of fleeing as was expected. And so on, excuse after excuse. After listening with growing impatience, Napoleon finally interrupted, and said: 'It would appear, gentlemen, that on this occasion you were very unlucky.' – 'Oui, mon Empereur,' they said, 'luck was not on our side.' – 'France,' remarked Napoleon, 'cannot afford unlucky generals.' And he dismissed them all.

Industry cannot afford unlucky managers if it is to remain competitive, and contribute in full measure to economic prosperity. As we have seen in the previous chapter, prosperity is a function of the national income per head of the population.

When politicians predict hopefully that their party will double the

34

standard of living of the country in twenty years, they mean that the average income per head, in real terms, will double over that period of time. They generally omit 'in real terms' from any statement made, as this might make their promises rather more difficult to achieve.

A nation can increase the national income per head in two ways:

1. By increasing the percentage of the population going out to work;
2. By increasing labour productivity.

In February 1963 the National Economic Development Council approved a 4 per cent growth objective for the British economy. This objective was further defined as a 4 per cent increase per annum in the Gross Domestic Product of the nation. In turn, the Gross Domestic Product, or G.D.P., was defined as the nation's total output of goods and services valued at market prices.

The N.E.D.C. report estimated that the 4 per cent growth objective could be achieved by an increase in the working population of 0·8 per cent, and an increase in labour productivity of 3·2 per cent per annum. The forecast was optimistic regarding the growth of the numbers employed, but not significantly so. The achievement of the plan thus depended, fairly and squarely, on the achievement of a 3·2 per cent per annum compound increase in productivity.

National productivity can be measured by comparing the output of the economy, in goods and services, with the man-hours required for the creation of this output. Referring again to Chapter 2, and the flow of money in the economy, we can say that the national income, excluding capital depreciation, is the sum of:

(a) The Gross Domestic Product;
    and
(b) Net incomes from abroad.

To increase the national income we can increase either (a) or (b). Incomes from abroad are a small proportion of the total, and in practice about 98 per cent of the national income is contributed by the G.D.P. Thus an increase in national prosperity primarily results from an increase in the G.D.P., and this, in its turn, results from an increase in the productivity of labour. Unless this latter occurs the economy will stagnate, and become progressively less competitive in the international markets of the world.

The relationship between national prosperity and labour productivity can perhaps best be expressed by a series of equations as follows:

$$\text{National Prosperity} = \frac{\text{National Income}}{\text{Total Population}} \qquad \text{(i)}$$

Now the total population is, for all practical purposes, a constant function of the working population. In the United Kingdom the constant is 2·25, and over many years has not varied from this figure by more than ±2 per cent.

Thus rewriting (i) we have:

$$\text{National Prosperity} = \frac{\text{National Income}}{K \times \text{Working Population}} \qquad \text{(ii)}$$

The national income is made up of the *G.D.P.* plus incomes from abroad, *Ia*, and so, if the working population is represented by *W*:

$$\text{National Income} = (G.D.P. + Ia) \qquad \text{(iii)}$$

∴

$$\text{National Prosperity} = \frac{(G.D.P. + Ia)}{\text{Working Population}}$$

$$\frac{G.D.P.}{W} + \frac{Ia}{W}$$

We can neglect the small term $\dfrac{Ia}{W}$ so that:

$$\text{National prosperity} = \frac{G.D.P.}{W} \qquad \text{(iv)}$$

From (iv) we can see that the prosperity of a country is determined primarily by the *G.D.P.* per head of the working population, since the ratio of working population to total population is reasonably constant in any particular country over a period of time. In other words, prosperity is determined by labour productivity.

It is customary among economists to measure a country's prosperity in terms of *annual* income per head. Prosperity would therefore increase by 50 per cent if the trade unions insisted that material comforts were all important, and decreed that the working population should work sixty hours per week rather than forty, thus producing 50 per cent more output in a year. Could one therefore say that productivity had increased by this amount? One could not! Output per man-hour would have remained unchanged, even although output per man-year increased by 50 per cent.

The incorrect inferences which can be drawn by a comparison of output per man-year are evident from the preceding example. Wherever possible, man-hours should be used for the measure of labour input. Unfortunately most published statistics relate to man-years. If man-years form the basis for comparisons, care must be taken to correct for variations in annual hours of work.

Labour productivity and capital productivity are two important measures of resource utilization. The efficiency of a company is generally quoted in terms of the profit it makes per unit of capital employed. Yet, in spite of this emphasis on return on capital, the productivity of capital has little immediate effect on the national income. It is the productivity of labour which is all-important.

As has been mentioned, the 1963 N.E.D.C. report forecast that labour productivity, in terms of annual output per worker, would rise at the rate of 3·2 per cent over a five-year period to 1966. In conjunction with an increase in numbers employed of 0·8 per cent, the overall growth rate would then be 4 per cent per annum. The target of a 3·2 per cent productivity increase was perfectly justified in terms of what *could* be achieved; it certainly was not justified in terms of what the United Kingdom economy *had* achieved over the past hundred years. In fact, even in the great days of the Victorian industrialists in the last fifty years of the nineteenth century, productivity rose by more than 3.2 per cent per annum in only a few isolated years.

Table 2 shows the changes which have occurred in output per head in the United Kingdom economy since 1963, together with the movement in incomes over the same period.

TABLE 2: % INCREASE PER ANNUM

	Output per Head	Income from Employment
1963	3·3	5·1
1964	4·9	8·3
1965	1·6	7·9
1966	2·0	7·0
1967	3·2	3·8
1968	4·7	7·0

Source: London and Cambridge Economic Bulletin

37

Over the six years covered in Table 2, the *average* annual increase in productivity coincided closely with the N.E.D.C. estimate, and all credit must be given to the accuracy of the original forecast. Forecast apart, the rate of growth in productivity, while satisfactory by the past standards of the United Kingdom economy, was most unsatisfactory when compared with the results of international competitors. Admittedly, it is always much easier to increase at a high rate when one is starting from a lower base, but even so this excuse cannot really be accepted if one looks at Britain's continued poor performance.

Table 3 shows the rate of growth of industrial production in a number of countries throughout the world. All the countries mentioned are major trading competitors of the United Kingdom, even although none of them is quite so reliant on foreign trade for maintaining national prosperity as the United Kingdom, with the possible exception of Japan.

TABLE 3: INDUSTRIAL PRODUCTION: GROWTH RATES

	1951–56 % p.a.	1956–60 % p.a.	1960–66 % p.a.
Japan	15·0	14·0	12·4
West Germany	11·2	6·3	5·7
Italy	8·3	7·7	8·1
France	5·7	5·2	5·2
United States	4·7	2·2	5·8
United Kingdom	3·2	2·4	3·5

Source: Econtel Research Limited

Over the twenty-year period from 1950 to 1970, the average rate of growth of industrial production in the United Kingdom was almost exactly 3 per cent per annum. When one considers that countries like Canada, Australia, New Zealand and Sweden averaged over 5 per cent, one is bound to conclude, in the words of the bard of Avon, that 'there is something rotten in the state of Denmark'. (For the record, Denmark showed a trend growth of 5½ per cent.)

We have seen that a good measure of national output is the Gross Domestic Product. Productivity is an output : input relationship. It must not be confused with production, which simply means 'that which has been produced', irrespective of the resource input. Productivity is output per unit of input, whether of labour, capital, raw material or other resource. Conventionally, the word 'productivity', without a prefix, refers to the productivity of labour, and this is the sense in which it will be used in the ensuing chapters. The productivity of other factors of production will be specifically defined, such as Productivity of Capital or Productivity of Floor Space.

It will be appreciated that productivity measurement is not an arithmetically exact science. One can never prove that the national productivity, or an industry's productivity, has risen by exactly x per cent over a year. For that matter, one can never prove that the profits of a company have risen by exactly y per cent over a period of time. The profit and loss account may say so, but there are certain matters which must be taken into account before arriving at a profit, and one cannot be arithmetically exact about these. For example, no profit can be declared without valuing stocks. As no one has yet produced the perfect mathematical formula for stock valuation, different people have different ideas as to the treatment of stocks in the balance sheet.

The judgment of different people can result in a different profit calculation – as was evident in the case of the Pergamon Press 1968 accounts. It will be recalled that these accounts showed trading profits and net assets of some £2 million and £7 million respectively. Following the withdrawal of an offer for Pergamon by the Leasco Data Processing Corporation, an independent firm of accountants was invited to give an opinion regarding the 1968 results.

The accountants' provisional conclusions were published early in 1970, and included the following comments:

'After taking account of the adjustments which we now recommend, the trading profits would not be more than £1,094,000.'
'The net assets at December 31, 1968, would be £4,729,000 compared with the £7,034,000 shown in the published accounts.'

The Pergamon case is an example of the fact that profitability is based on a number of assumptions. As Robert Maxwell, the founder and erstwhile chief executive of Pergamon, pointed out, a reduction in the profits of the amount recommended was well within the margins to be expected when reporting accountants applied different accounting principles.

There is, then, no mathematically correct measure of profitability. This certainly does not imply that one cannot assess profits. What it does imply is that the basic assumptions must be defined and understood, and that one must be consistent in the treatment of expenses,

stock valuations and so on, taking one year with another. Having
defined the principles to be adopted, these must be applied in a con-
scientious manner in order to obtain a true and fair measure of performance. As with profits so with productivity.

Accepting that productivity is an output : input relationship, how
then does one measure the output of a company? The 1963 N.E.D.C.
report examined a number of industries in depth, and it is interesting
to review the measures of output used for these different industries.
Table 4 gives details of some of the measurement units which were
selected.

TABLE 4

Industry	Measure of Output	Unit
Coal	Physical Output	Tons
Electricity	Power	Kilowatt Hours
Gas	Net Output	£ sterling
Petroleum	Refinery Output	Tons
Chocolate	Physical Output	Tons
Iron and steel	Physical Output	Tons
Machine tools	Sales value, 1961 Prices	£ sterling
Heavy electrical machines	Sales value, 1961 Prices	£ sterling
Electronics	Sales value, 1961 Prices	£ sterling
Motor vehicles	Number of Vehicles	Thousands

Source: N.E.D.C. Report: February, 1963

The golden rule of productivity measurement is to select the most
meaningful measure of output, and then to equate this to the input of
resources. If tons are a good measure, then tons should be used. If
number of vehicles, then number of vehicles. If sales value, then sales
value. Unfortunately for the analyst, it is rare that tons, or vehicles, or
sales value are good measures. There is always the problem of differing
product mix, resulting in the question 'Tons of what?' or 'Sales of
what?' A company manufacturing gold cuff-links is likely to find that
its output, in terms of sales value, is drastically reduced if the general
public suddenly decides that it wishes to buy silver cuff-links instead.
It does not follow that its productivity would have reduced correspondingly, as might be incorrectly inferred from a study of the annual
sales per employee.

Although the value of sales does not represent the output of a
company, nevertheless it can, in certain circumstances, be useful to

express productivity in terms of sales value per employee. Provided that raw material costs are reasonably consistent across a number of firms within an industry, then a comparison of sales per employee can be a helpful indication of resource utilization. This method of comparison has the great advantage that the figures are readily available from published information, which is certainly not the case with more sophisticated and accurate measures of output such as Added Value.

A typical productivity comparison between a number of motor car firms is shown in Figure 4. This would appear to indicate that the giant car companies in the U.S.A., with annual sales of some £13,000 to £14,000 per employee, have a productivity two and a half times that of their European competitors. In fact, independent assessments have come to the same conclusion, and this is a good instance of the fact that, within an industry, annual sales per employee can be a simple and reasonably effective measure of productivity.

FIGURE 4

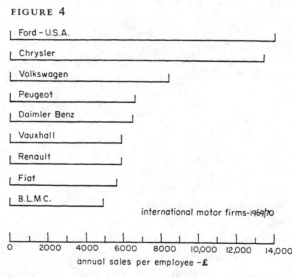

Most people are aware of the relationship between productivity and capital investment. The higher the capital per employee, the higher the labour productivity.

To illustrate the type of comparison which can be made by examining sales per employee, and capital per employee, a number of companies in the United Kingdom engineering sector have been analysed, as

41

shown in Table 5. Is there, one wonders, any significance in the fact that the two companies with the highest productivity both have American antecedents?

TABLE 5

	Annual Sales per Employee – £	Capital Employed* per Employee – £
Caterpillar Tractor	8,300	6,000
Hoover	6,400	4,400
British Ropes	4,650	3,650
Metal Closures	4,500	2,400
Tube Investments	4,100	3,350
G.K.N.	4,000	2,940
Vickers	3,900	2,900
Hawker Siddeley	3,900	2,140
Weir Group	3,800	2,700
Birmid	3,750	2,150
Rolls-Royce	3,750	2,550
David Brown	3,350	1,740
Lesney Products	3,250	1,640
Clayton Dewandre	3,200	2,360
Dowty Group	3,150	2,250
Joseph Lucas	3,100	1,540
Associated Engineering	2,700	2,100

* Total Tangible Assets less Current Liabilities

Source: The Times 500, 1969–70

If we plot productivity, in terms of Sales per Employee, against Capital per Employee for the companies quoted in Table 5, we obtain a graph as shown in Figure 5. Whilst one normally expects to find a linear relationship, the slope of the line does vary from industry to industry, depending on the amount of capital which has to be injected in order to replace one man.

For any given industry, one would anticipate finding an appreciable scatter of individual companies about the average line, since companies can be more or less efficient in their use of labour, and more or less efficient in their use of capital. For example, a company might deviate appreciably from the average simply because it was carrying very large stock inventories, thus showing an apparently high capital intensity without any correspondingly high productivity. Alternatively, a company might be operating with very old machinery in rented buildings, thus showing a low capital intensity against an average labour productivity. There have been instances where this latter situation has applied, although it is more usual for companies operating old and well written down machines to have a low productivity. Modern methods and modern machines are normally an essential component of higher productivity.

The 1967 Companies Act, which ruled that companies must publish their sales turnover in the annual accounts, was of great assistance to those wishing to examine in some detail the performance of a given

FIGURE 5

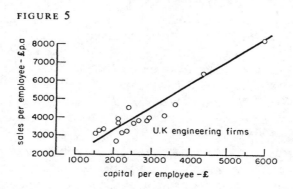

company. Admittedly, many people considered that the Act was a gross impertinence, which indeed it was in those clauses which required the salary of the chief executive to be revealed, as well as the salary bands of all other directors. These clauses bore the signs of an envious society, and were hardly necessary to enable shareholders to judge the quality and standing of their investment. Nevertheless the ruling about divulging sales turnover was a good one. In spite of all the protestations which were made before the Act, there is no shred of evidence to suggest that a company is revealing a deep trade secret to its competitors by quoting its turnover. Nor is there any evidence that it is thereby made less competitive.

The 1967 Companies Act has made it possible to compare the productivity of firms in terms of annual sales per employee. There are many potential lessons to be learned from such comparisons, but the impact of these is somewhat reduced by the fact that sales turnover is not a good measure of output. Sales turnover can increase rapidly for no reason other than a rise in raw materials costs. A company producing copper fittings would have shown a startling increase in turnover between

November 1968 and November 1969, and a similar startling increase in sales per employee. Hypothetically, the Chairman of such a company might have remarked that his company had, by vigorous application of dynamic management techniques, achieved a record increase in sales over the twelve months ending November 1969. In fact, over this twelve months, the price of copper rose from £450 per ton to £675 per ton, or 50 per cent. Such an increase in raw materials costs would almost certainly increase the sales turnover – assuming that the sales manager remembered to increase prices – by about 25 per cent. By no stretch of the imagination could the higher sales turnover be attributed to an improvement in the efficiency of the company.

It would be foolish to suggest that one should never judge a company's performance on the basis of sales ratios. Profit, labour costs, fixed overheads, and capital employed are commonly expressed in terms of sales value. Yet, equally, one must be aware of the limitations of such judgments, as instanced by the example of the imaginary company manufacturing copper fittings.

It has already been stated that productivity measurement is not an exact science. Nevertheless systematic measurement can play an important part in the control of a company, particularly in the assessment of the efficiency of resource utilization. In his book* *The Practice of Management*, Peter Drucker commented that, since the resources available to them are generally similar, the only thing that differentiates one business from another in any given field is the quality of management at all levels. He continued: 'A productivity measurement is the only yardstick that can actually gauge the competence of management, and allow comparison between managements of different units within the enterprise, and of different enterprises.'

To measure productivity we must be able to measure output. This is a subject we shall discuss further in the next chapter.

* Heinemann 1955.

Chapter 5

The Added Value Concept

It used to be said, perhaps with some justification, that British industry was managed by a collection of gifted amateurs. How such a tradition arose is somewhat of a mystery (the playing fields of Eton?) since there is ample evidence to show that the successful industrialists of past and present have been hard-headed, professional men.

The 1960s saw a growing awareness of the need for trained men to staff the senior positions in industry. After all, as the chief executive of a multi-million pound company remarked at the Administrative Staff College, Henley on Thames, in 1968, one does not entrust one's health to a doctor who has no medical qualifications. Why then should one entrust the management of a company to a man with no managerial qualifications?

In no field is professionalism more necessary than that of company appraisal and control. The amateur may be able to control a company, more or less efficiently, by intuition. That there are people with a well-developed ability to make the correct decision apparently by intuition is indisputable. One cannot discount intuition when it is a matter of locating opportunities – at best, an abstract technique. When one is concerned with concrete matters, such as the measurement of company performance, intuition has (or should have) very little part to play.

In any field of activity, those who wish to succeed frequently spend considerable time in studying, discussing, imitating, and learning from others who are recognized masters of their trade. Consider, for example, the tremendous interest generated in the golfing fraternity by television programmes showing Jack Nicklaus in action. No true golfer could ever watch a master player in action without feeling that he has gained several ideas. The careful observance of the real expert can well result in at least some of the expertise rubbing off on the observer.

What is true for golf holds equally true for football, tennis, bridge, and every other field of human activity. It also holds true in the field of management, which is one notable reason why good management breeds good managers, and bad management breeds bad managers. Management quality tends to perpetuate itself, possibly through contiguity and conditioning. It is the boss's behavioural patterns which set the style of management within a company, just as it is the parent's behaviour which conditions the characteristics of the growing child.

It is always instructive to study the expert. How then does the real professional appraiser judge the performance of a company?

In 1968 *The Times* published an article describing how Arnold Weinstock used a number of key ratios for assessing the performance of G.E.C. There were seven ratios, which were:

1. Profit : Sales
2. Profit : Capital Employed
3. Profit per Employee
4. Sales : Capital Employed
5. Sales : Stocks
6. Sales : Fixed Assets
7. Sales per Employee

With the exception of 1 above, it will be noted that the remaining ratios represent output : input, or are intended to do so. Any ratio which includes profit must of course be related to the level of activity, since profit is volume sensitive. This applies to ratios 1–3, which are virtually meaningless without any adjustment (that is, flexing) for changes in activity. Nevertheless the intention behind these ratios is to assess the ultimate output, namely profit, in relation to the level of sales, capital employed, and number of employees.

Ratios 4–7 are productivity ratios, for the purpose of assessing the productivity of capital, of stocks, of fixed assets, and of labour. The difficulty here is that the sales value of a company does not strictly represent its output, as has already been mentioned in Chapter 4. Indeed, the comparison of disparate companies using sales ratios is almost meaningless, although such ratios do have a use for examining trends within a given firm provided that the type of product and raw material costs do not alter appreciably.

The Weinstock control ratios are extremely interesting, and they undoubtedly enable changes to be identified in levels of performance within a given company. However, they have certain disadvantages if one is attempting to compare performance across a number of different companies, due to the limitations of sales value as a measure of output.

While it has been recognized for many years that sales value is not an adequate measure, it is only comparatively recently that the concept of using Added Value to represent the net output of a company has been developed as a management technique.

At this point we must ask why it is that Added Value represents net output. Unless the answer is fully understood and accepted, the application of Added Value ratios to company appraisal and control will never be fully effective.

If we revert to a basic law of economics that the value of all incomes equals the value of all output, we will see that, if we can only define a company's net income, we shall also be able to define its net output. Let us then look at the incomes generated from a series of transactions starting with firm A. A extracts iron ore from the ground, and converts it into pig iron which it sells to B. Using this pig iron as its raw material, B converts this into steel which it sells to C. C then fabricates the steel into (say) a refrigerator which it sells to D, the final consumer.

Starting with A, who buys no raw material, simply extracting iron ore from the ground, we can see that B's raw material is pig iron, and C's is steel. Further, to convert iron ore, pig iron and steel into a product suitable for the next purchaser in the chain, A, B and C must buy from outside suppliers such essentials as electric power, tools, consumable stores and so on. We will define these as outside purchases. By allocating some typical costs to each firm, we can now look further into the matter of defining company income.

A company's operating costs may be classified as Raw Materials, Purchases, Production Labour, and Fixed Expenses. Using these four categories we can allocate the costs as shown in Table 6. (The term 'Purchases' includes the cost of all bought-out items classified as a variable expense, such as tools, process power, carriage outwards, etc.)

It is evident from Table 6 that the total company incomes do not consist of the sum of the individual sales values. Total incomes do not amount to £900, even although this might, at first sight, seem to be the case. After all, A sells to B for £100, B to C for £300, and C to D for £500. However, a moment's reflection will show that the combined incomes are not £900. The £300 received by B from C includes an element of £100, which represents the amount owed by B to A for the supply of pig iron. This £100 is not part of B's net income. It is partly A's income and partly the income of the outside suppliers. £90 is A's and £10 outside suppliers'.

TABLE 6: TRANSACTION INCOMES

	Company A	Company B	Company C	Company D
	\multicolumn{4}{c}{£ Sterling}			
Final Purchase Price				500
Raw Material	Nil	100	300	
Outside Purchases	10	20	20	
	10	120	320	
Labour and Fixed Expenses	80	150	130	
	90	270	450	
PROFIT	10	30	50	
Sales Value – Gross	100	300	500	
Gross Income	100	300	500	
Deduct Raw Material	Nil	100	300	
	100	200	200	
Deduct Outside Purchases	10	20	20	
Net Income	90	180	180	

Had we included the £100 in B's income, we would have counted it twice. Once in A's income, and again in B's. Similarly with the £500 received by C from D.

Examination of Table 6 shows clearly that the net income of A is £90, of B £180, and of C £180, a total of £450. This sum represents the total operating costs and profits of A, B, and C.

The sales revenue received by any company, then, is not entirely that company's income. Firstly it must pay for all the raw materials and other external purchases which it must make if it is to be enabled to carry on its business. It must have raw materials, unless it is an extractive industry. It must have tools, power, water, etc., if it is to have the wherewithal to enable it to convert raw materials from one form to another. The fact that C's income of £500 contains an element of £320 which C owes to its suppliers is a result of the necessities of book-keeping. It would make no difference financially if C were to issue a two-part invoice to D, requesting that D pay C the sum of £180, and that D pay C's suppliers £320. Financially it would make no difference, although the mind boggles at the clerical efforts necessary to make such a situation workable.

For reasons of simplicity, a purchaser pays only one creditor when he buys a given product. It is up to the creditor to pay, from the revenue received, the one hundred and one suppliers who have contributed to the product. Only when these suppliers have been paid can the original creditor use the remaining sum of money to pay for his own operating costs. This residual represents his net income. From this he must pay the wages and salaries of his employees, his rent, rates, depreciation, and other fixed expenses and, if any is left, make a profit. This net income, which is the sum of money remaining after all outside purchases have been deducted from the sales revenue, is the Added Value of the firm. In other words:

Sales—(Raw Materials+Outside Purchases) = Added Value

The Added Value is the net income of a company. It is also the net output. The Added Value represents a company's contribution to the Gross Domestic Product. The efficiency with which the management of a company combines the resources needed for the creation of Added Value is thus a matter of paramount importance, not only to the company itself, but also to the nation.

The concept of Added Value is not easy to understand, particularly since the term is not in general use in accounting circles. It may therefore be helpful at this stage to enlarge on this subject, since if it is not fully understood much of the ensuing discussion will have limited relevance.

Added Value is the net income, and thus the net output, of a firm. It constitutes the fund from which all the operating expenses of the company must be paid after making provision for the purchase of raw materials and other external purchases.

49

A typical company profit and loss account could be written as follows:

TABLE 7: PROFIT AND LOSS ACCOUNT – MARGINAL

A B C Limited	Year to 31st December 1970		P & L Account
	£	£	%
Sales (net)		1,000,000	100·0
Less Raw Materials	560,000		
Production Labour	120,000		
Purchases	80,000	760,000	76·0
Contribution		240,000	24·0
Less Rent and Rates			
Building Maintenance			
Bad Debts			
Depreciation			
All other Fixed		140,000	14·0
Net Profit (pre Tax)		100,000	10·0

Table 7 is presented in marginal form. It will be noted that this presentation does not include an element of stock valuation at the start or finish of the accounting period. The underlying principle of marginal costing is that the operating expenses and raw material costs should be equated to the level of sales achieved. The emphasis is on sales, and the expenses incurred in making these sales.

Those who have studied the basic principles leading to the analysis of company income and output may find it strange that the conventional marginal profit and loss layout does not indicate clearly and objectively the net income of the company. For that matter, neither does the conventional profit and loss layout, with its allowance for opening and closing stock valuations. Surely the single most important piece of information which the top management of a company must know is its net income? Fortunately, there is no difficulty in providing this information. We merely rewrite Table 7, as shown in Table 8.

The net income of A.B.C. Limited is the Added Value; this is also the net output. The relationships are readily seen to be:

Sales—(Raw Materials+Purchases) = Added Value
Net Profit+Fixed Expenses+Labour = Added Value
Contribution+Labour   = Added Value

TABLE 8: PROFIT AND LOSS ACCOUNT – NET INCOME

A B C Limited	Year to 31st December 1970	P & L Account
	£	%
Sales (net)	1,000,000	100·0
Raw Materials	560,000	56·0
	440,000	44·0
External Purchases	80,000	8·0
Added Value (Net Income)	360,000	36·0
Production labour	120,000	12·0
Contribution	240,000	24·0
Fixed Expenses	140,000	14·0
Net Profit (pre Tax)	100,000	10·0

Assuming that fixed expenses remain fixed, irrespective of sales volume, then a company will maximize its profits by maximizing Added Value as a percentage of Sales, and minimizing Production Labour as a percentage of Added Value.

A company is in business, apart from social and ethical considerations, to create Added Value. If the directors of a company were able to create Added Value by going into a trance, by borrowing long and lending short, by painting artistic masterpieces, or by any other means, they would no doubt do so. As it happens, of course, none of these methods would, in fact, create much Added Value for their company. What happens, therefore, is that the directors can only make a satisfactory income for the company by the efficient use of the resources available to the company. These resources may be manual skills, technical skills, accumulated know-how, special purpose machines, factory layout, or any one of a number of characteristics which provide their company with something special to offer in the market place. It is the resources at its disposal which enable a company to create a profit.

From Table 8 we can derive the break-even sales of A.B.C. Limited. Break-even sales are defined as the level of sales at which a company makes neither a profit or a loss. In other words, it breaks even in its transactions. At a sales value equal to the break-even, the fixed expenses of the company are exactly offset by the contribution associated with this level of sales.

To illustrate this point, Table 8 shows that the fixed expenses of A.B.C. Limited are £140,000 per annum. The contribution to fixed overheads for each £100 of sales is £24. Thus the value of sales needed to absorb £140,000 fixed expenses is £140,000 ÷ £24 × 100, or £583,333. To quote a figure as accurately as this is quite ridiculous in practice, since it is calculated on a number of assumptions. Let us therefore say that the break-even sales are £590,000. If the value of sales of A.B.C. Limited is less than £590,000, the company will make a loss. If the value of sales is greater than £590,000, the company will make a profit. The amount of profit (assuming the costs are correct) will be £24 for each £100 of sales in excess of the break-even.

Most professional managers are familiar with the layout of a conventional break-even chart. This is shown in Figure 6.

FIGURE 6: CONVENTIONAL BREAK-EVEN CHART – A.B.C. LIMITED

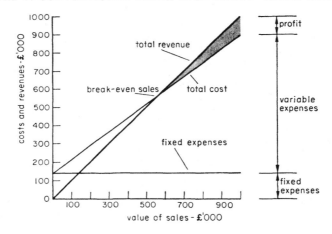

The conventional chart shows the relationship between Sales revenues and Total Costs (made up of fixed and variable expenses). This type of chart is perfectly adequate for providing a visual presentation of the break-even. Note that, at the break-even point, Sales Revenue is equal to Variable plus Fixed Expenses. However, for those who wish to consider, in greater detail, the creation of Added Value, and the constituents of total cost in terms of raw material, purchases, labour and fixed expenses, we can construct an Added Value break-even chart, as shown in Figure 7.

Figure 7 indicates that Added Value is created as soon as the company makes a sale. The amount of Added Value increases in direct proportion to the value of sales, and the greater the Added Value as a percentage of sales, the lower will be the break-even. Note that, at the break-even point, Sales Revenue is equal to Added Value plus Purchases plus Raw Material Costs.

The level of sales at which a company breaks even is a matter of extreme importance to those charged with the responsibility of managing the business. As a general rule, companies with high fixed expenses have a high break-even ratio (that is, break-even sales : sales at capacity output). Companies with low fixed expenses have a low break-even ratio. However, high-fixed-expense companies tend to be highly capitalized, with a correspondingly high productivity. The reverse

FIGURE 7: ADDED VALUE BREAK-EVEN CHART — A.B.C. LIMITED

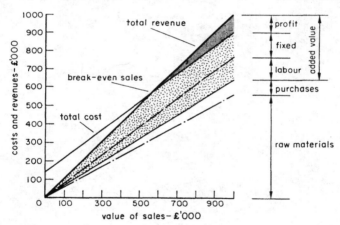

applies to low-fixed-expense companies. Consequently the former tend to make more profit than the latter per £100 of sales in excess of the break-even. However, they are also more vulnerable to a reduction in sales volume, and could typically make a loss when running at 70 per cent of capacity, whereas a low-fixed-expense company could well still make a profit at 50 per cent of capacity.

Break-even charts are useful in that they assist one to visualize cost and revenue relationships. In practice, however, there is no need to draw a chart to obtain the break-even sales. These can most conveniently be calculated by dividing the fixed expenses by the rate of contribution (as a percentage of sales).

Irrespective of its method of computation, the break-even point is of considerable relevance in the assessment of company performance. The break-even sales figure, and its relationship to actual sales and capacity sales figures, are statistics which should be submitted to top management at least on a monthly basis. An increase in the break-even is the result either of an increase in fixed expenses, a reduction in the rate of contribution, or a combination of both. Whatever the reason, an investigation should immediately be made to find out the reason since, unless corrective action is taken, profits will be adversely affected.

In this chapter we have discussed the derivation of Added Value, and its meaningfulness as the measure of company income and output. In the following chapter we shall examine the application of Added Value to productivity measurement, and subsequently to the overall field of company performance appraisal and control.

Chapter 6

The Productivity of Labour

During the 1960s many eminent observers of the industrial scene expressed grave concern at the growing size of large international corporations, and at the power of the men who headed them. That such men could make decisions which might affect the lives and prosperity of many thousands of people, in countries remote from corporation headquarters, was a possibility which they felt could scarcely be viewed with equanimity.

Jacques Servan-Schreiber, in his book, *The American Challenge*, pointed out that, by the 1980s the third greatest industrial power in the world, after the United States and Russia, might well be American industry in Europe. (Judging by the recent scale of American investment in Europe, this forecast could easily prove to be correct.)

There is no doubt that a large international corporation is in a position to influence both the economic health and the social patterns of a country. For example, the well-known British company of Booker Bros. operates sugar planations in South America, and also has an interest in James Bond books. Many thousands of people rely on the sugar plantations for their livelihood, but it is quite possible that the profitability of sugar is vastly less than the profitability resulting from the escapades of 007. The human suffering which could result from Booker Bros. deciding to concentrate on the world of books to the exclusion of the world of sugar can readily be imagined.

That Booker Bros., who have for many years been renowned for their sense of social responsibility, would be unlikely to maximize their profits without full consideration of the human implications is a matter which does not satisfy the critics of big business. After all, they argue, history shows that men in a position of absolute power have tended to use that power absolutely, in the sure conviction that the end justifies the means. The man who has reached the top tends to be convinced, often with some justification, that he has succeeded because of his abilities, sense of judgment, and capacity for being right more often than wrong. Fortified with this conviction, he may well take decisions in the pursuit of an objective, irrespective of the effect of such decisions on society.

The international corporation inevitably affects a nation's prosperity. The taxes it pays, the investments made, the employment generated, the profits remitted back to headquarters, all have an impact on the economy. If the Ford Motor Company decides to increase investment in Germany, and reduce activities in Britain, thousands of Germans and thousands of Britons will be affected whether they like it or not. Similarly with Britain and Italy in the case of Dunlop-Pirelli, or France and Britain in the case of Chrysler. Of course, there are those who are of the belief that they will be able to influence the International Trade Union movement to the extent that workers in one country will refuse to accept benefits if these are to be gained at the expense of their brothers in another country. Perhaps one day this will happen. In the meantime one can only record that there seems to be a general reluctance on anyone's part to reject an opportunity for gain, even though such a gain is at someone else's expense. One of the main arguments against group incentive schemes has always been that the bad penalize the good, that is, that the below average reduce the bonus earned by the above average. Few people ever accept that they are below average, as is instanced by a recent poll of Chicago motorists, where 91 per cent considered that their driving ability was above average!

For all his veneer of civilization, man is not very far removed from the Darwinian world of the survival of the fittest. Few people are prepared to shed a tear for those who are unwilling to pull their weight; few people are prepared to forego material advantages just for the sake of equal misery for all; few companies are prepared to refrain from action, irrespective of the social implications, if they genuinely believe that the economic health of their company is being endangered.

Internationalism will undoubtedly be a feature of the industrial life of the 1970s, and one of the interesting by-products of such internationalism has been the need for an evaluation of the operating

56

efficiencies of companies located in different countries. Such an evaluation must obviously include scrutiny of resource utilization, and in this context the Group Services Manager of one of Britain's leading aluminium companies has frequently stated that the only worthwhile procedure yet devised for international productivity comparisons is through an assessment of Added Value ratios. No other method provides a measure sufficiently valid for appraising companies in different parts of the world: no other measure is so meaningful for comparing wage and salary costs per unit of output.

Labour productivity is perhaps best expressed in terms of Added Value per man-hour. Unfortunately for the analyst, companies do not publish statistics regarding man-hours worked, nor for that matter do they quote their annual Added Value. The 1967 Companies Act was very helpful in its statutory requirements for revealing numbers employed, annual sales value, and wage and salary bill, but for some strange reason the most important statistic of all, namely the net output or Added Value of the Company, was omitted. Perhaps it was decided that the publication of Added Value might have provided shareholders with too powerful a weapon for appraising the effectiveness of their company and its management!

For control purposes within a company, the Added Value per man-hour should always be used for the examination of productivity and productivity trends. When examining the performance of British industry as a whole, we have to rely on an analysis of Added Value per man-year, the primary source of comparative information being the Census of Production reports. However, before quoting from these reports, it is advisable that we are quite clear *why* productivity measurement is important.

In 1965 the National Industrial Conference Board – a non-profit, fact-finding organization in the United States – published a handbook entitled *Measuring Company Productivity*. In this, the comment was made that managements have been slow to institute measures of productivity performance, possibly due to scepticism as to the usefulness of such measures. In addition, it was remarked that there were instances where companies had reservations as to the accuracy of the measures themselves, in spite of the fact that the underlying assumptions were no more arbitrary than those used in the preparation of company accounts.

57

The N.I.C.B. handbook concluded that there was a real and positive value to be gained from productivity measurement. 'A regular and systematic evaluation of productivity trends, and changes in trends, can provide management with another reference point for viewing profits, and for taking corrective action before it is too late.'*

Companies who have had experience in the field of productivity measurement will say that the first essential is to check their performance against that of other companies in the same industry. This is a valuable exercise, since most company managements are perpetually concerned about inefficiency. However, since resources are always limited, it is necessary to focus attention on specific areas of inefficiency rather than dissipate efforts over a wide front. Interfirm comparisons can often be most helpful in locating these specific areas, and it is perhaps regrettable that industry does not make more use of the facilities which are available for this purpose.

While it is true to say that only a relatively few firms participate in an exchange of operating ratios, mainly through their Trade Associations or, in Britain, through the British Institute of Management, every company is able to assess its productivity by analysing Census of Production reports. The Census, which is made every five years for all industrial firms, contains much valuable information concerning the operating efficiency of British industry, and includes statistics on the number and size of establishments, sales value, added value, stock levels, numbers employed, and wages and salaries.

In Chapter 4 it was suggested that a simple and reasonably effective measure of labour productivity could be obtained by using sales value as the output and number of employees as the input. In other words, annual sales value per employee. A more sophisticated and considerably more accurate measure results from using Added Value as the output and number of employees as the input. Table 9 shows both these methods, the statistics relating to a selection of nine industry groups.

If we now rewrite Table 9, expressing the output/input relationships in terms of indices, taking Shipbuilding as 100, we obtain Table 10.

From Table 10 it will be noted that there is a considerable discrepancy between the indices quoted in column A and those quoted in column B. Which then is right? To a certain extent both are, since each

* *Measuring Company Productivity*, New York, N.I.C.B., 1965.

TABLE 9: OUTPUT PER EMPLOYEE 1968

Industry Groups	Annual Sales per Employee – £	Annual Added Value per Employee – £
Copper and Brass Manufacture	12,300	2,285
General Chemicals	10,200	3,935
Cement	7,500	3,520
Iron and Steel	6,300	1,950
Motor Vehicles	5,900	2,135
Mechanical Engineering	3,800	2,000
Electrical Engineering	3,600	1,825
Radio and Radar	3,300	1,895
Shipbuilding	2,900	1,585

Source: Census of Production 1968 (Provisional)

TABLE 10: PRODUCTIVITY INDICES 1968

Industry Groups	A Productivity Index (Basis: Sales per Employee)	B Productivity Index (Basis: A.V. per Employee)
Copper and Brass Manufacture	424	144
General Chemicals	352	248
Cement	258	221
Iron and Steel	217	122
Motor Vehicles	204	134
Mechanical Engineering	131	126
Electrical Engineering	124	115
Radio and Radar	114	119
Shipbuilding	100	100

Source: Census of Production 1968

is a productivity measure using different units. However, column B is likely to be more realistic than column A, as the validity of A is seriously impaired due to the effect of raw material costs.

Sales Value is the sum of Raw Material costs, purchases, labour, Fixed Expenses and Profit. Or, expressed another way, it is the sum of Raw Material Costs, Purchases and Added Value. It is perfectly possible for two different industries to produce the same Added Value per employee. Indeed, if we compare the net output per employee of Copper and Brass with Mechanical Engineering, it will be noted from Table 9 that each industry is within 6½ per cent of the mean of the two combined. However, the Copper and Brass manufacturers are working with raw material costing some £500–550 per ton (in 1968) as compared with the Mechanical Engineering industry which was converting mainly ferrous materials, costing some £100 per ton in the part-processed condition. A difference in raw material costs of this magnitude would produce differences in Sales per employee of the order of those shown in Table 9.

Another useful exercise is to compare the changes in Sales per employee and Added Value per employee since 1963. These are shown in Table 11.

TABLE 11: PRODUCTIVITY CHANGES 1963–1968 – INDUSTRY GROUPS

Industry Groups	A Annual Sales per Employee – £			B Annual Added Value per Employee – £		
	1963	1968	Change %	1963	1968	Change %
Copper and Brass Manufacture	6,700	12,300	+83	1,600	2,285	+43
General Chemicals	6,500	10,200	+57	2,860	3,935	+38
Cement	6,000	7,500	+25	2,870	3,520	+23
Iron and Steel	4,900	6,300	+28	1,505	1,950	+30
Motor Vehicles	4,700	5,900	+26	1,655	2,135	+29
Mechanical Engineering	2,600	3,800	+46	1,360	2,000	+47
Electrical Engineering	2,500	3,600	+44	1,245	1,825	+47
Radio and Radar	2,400	3,330	+38	1,410	1,895	+34
Shipbuilding	2,100	2,900	+38	1,080	1,585	+47

Source: Census of Production 1968

Table 11 is most revealing. It shows clearly those industries in which raw material costs have risen disproportionately over the years (Copper and General Chemicals) and the industry in which prices have not been increased in line with economic requirements (Shipbuilding). The remainder have not experienced any abnormal changes in raw material costs or selling prices between 1963 and 1968.

Table 11 shows that, in general terms, the net output per employee, in £ sterling, increased by 40 per cent over the five years to 1968. During this period the value of the £1 reduced by about 17 per cent. Thus the true increase in labour productivity – net output per head – was some 16 per cent, or just over 3 per cent per annum, compound rate.

Tables 9, 10, and 11 show how it is possible to compare labour productivity across a number of industries. The simplest method, for

which source information is readily available, is to make the comparison
in terms of annual sales per employee. The shortcomings of this method
have already been examined, and are not evident in the Added Value
approach.

Table 11 indicates that, when industries or firms are using different
raw materials, there is not a good correlation between changes in sales
and changes in Added Value over time. However, within a given
industry, where raw materials costs are likely to be broadly similar, the
correlation is very much better. This is illustrated in Table 12.

TABLE 12: PRODUCTIVITY CHANGES 1963–1968

Industry Sub-division	Annual Sales per Employee – £			Annual Added Value per Employee – £			
	1963	1968	Change %	1963	1968	Change %	Index
Earth Moving Equipment	4,000	6,400	+60	1,600	2,550	+60	160
Office Machinery	2,170	4,020	+85	1,250	2,175	+74	137
Textile Machinery	2,430	3,900	+60	1,325	2,100	+58	132
Industrial Engines	2,720	4,100	+51	1,250	1,955	+56	123
Mining Machinery	3,480	4,400	+26	1,505	1,945	+29	123
Refrigerating Machinery	3,280	4,100	+25	1,545	1,925	+25	121
Metal Working Machine Tools	2,640	3,500	+33	1,405	1,900	+35	119
Agricultural Machinery	3,270	4,450	+36	1,470	1,900	+30	119
Pumps, Valves, Compressors	2,600	3,650	+40	1,390	1,875	+35	118
Total Mech. Engineering	2,600	3,800	+46	1,360	2,000	+47	126

(Indices based on 1968 values. Base Industry = Shipbuilding = 100)

Source: Census of Production 1968

Sufficient has been said to show that productivity measurement,
through the adoption of Added Value as the common measure of output, can provide management with a reference point against which
future improvements can be assessed. The big question that remains is
how to improve productivity.

Improved productivity is the result of a large number of actions –
better methods, better planning, more mechanization, more skills etc.
But the key factors which will determine future prosperity are:

1. The amount and quality of investment.
2. The education and skill of the labour force.
3. The exploitation of technology.

It is difficult to say which of the above is the most important, any more than one can say which is the most important leg of a three-legged stool. Perhaps the easiest to quantify is that of investment. Many analyses have been made into the relationship between capital and labour productivity; investigating teams have reported that one reason for the high productivity in the U.S.A. is the amount of horse-power at the worker's elbow; countries which invest a great deal of their national income, like Japan, have shown a consistently high improvement in productivity over the years; and so on. That there is a

FIGURE 8: PRODUCTIVITY AND CAPITAL INVESTMENT

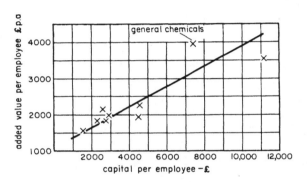

relationship between the amount and quality of capital available and productivity is indisputable. Unfortunately the census of Production does not give details of Capital Employed, perhaps to avoid arguments about differing methods of capital valuation. Thus to investigate the capital intensity of the industry groups quoted in Tables 9–11 (see Figure 8) it has been necessary to extract details of typical companies within these groups from their annual accounts, and to make the assumption that these are typical of the industry as a whole. The figures quoted represent the average results of four or five typical companies within each of the nine industry groups. It will be seen that there is a definite trend for productivity to increase with increasing capital per employee. In this respect the General Chemicals industry, showing £3,935 Added Value per Employee for £7,400 net assets per employee, is particularly good.

In this chapter we have discussed the measurement of labour productivity, and the relevance of Added Value in this area of management activity. In the next chapter we shall look at the relationships between pay and productivity, on the international, national and industry levels, and examine the allocation of a company's income between the factors of production.

Chapter 7

The Employee's Share of Company Income

The New Testament tells a story concerning a number of labourers who were hired, a few at a time, to work in a vineyard. The first group was engaged early in the morning, the second later in the morning, the third after lunch and so on. Each man agreed to work for the same sum of money, but when each was paid his due at the end of the shift there was, not unexpectedly, a furious row. Those who had worked through the heat of the day did not see why they should be paid the same as those who had only started in the afternoon; those who had started in the afternoon said that the wages had been freely negotiated and the contract should be honoured. Everyone argued with everyone else.

The fact that each and every man had agreed on a specific wage before accepting the work only increased the sense of injustice. There is nothing more calculated to make a man feel aggressive than to know he has made a bad bargain, unless it is the knowledge that someone else has made a better one.

The story of the labourers who were worthy of their hire is an early example of an industrial dispute on the subject of a fair day's pay. The labourers were not concerned with the ability of the vineyard owner to pay the money. They were concerned about the different rates of pay for doing the same job. On his part, the vineyard owner, although probably not worried about whether he could afford to pay the money, was very much concerned with a principle, namely that a free man who freely enters into a contract should abide by that contract.

Nowadays, of course, we are very much more sophisticated when arguing about wage levels than was the case with the tired and dusty labourers of the Bible story. There is also another very important difference. The difference is that the ability of a twentieth-century

64

company to pay an increased wage and remain competitive in international markets must always be of paramount importance. The important words here are *remain competitive in international markets*. In the home market alone, higher wages lead to higher prices once spare capacity has been utilized. But since wages are higher, people have more money (excepting the unfortunates on fixed incomes) and can pay the increased prices without reducing overall demand. Thus, within a domestic economy, higher wages alone do not directly affect a company's ability to pay.

The factor which is of over-riding priority to any company engaged in wage negotiations is its competitive ability. Losing competitive ability is a perpetual worry. Most companies exist in a non-monopolistic environment, and are reluctant to increase prices to recover the extra costs resulting from a wage increase. They hesitate to do so because they are afraid that their main competitors will be more efficient than they, or willing to accept less profit, and will thus absorb the higher wage rates without passing them on to their customers in the form of higher prices.

If all companies who had granted a wage increase agreed to raise their prices to cover the increase, no company could claim that it could not afford to pay. This, however, would hardly be likely to happen, as the more efficient companies would see the opportunity of gaining business at the expense of the less efficient, and would be unwilling to co-operate. Again, therefore, we return to a company's anxiety about losing its competitive ability when it is faced with an increase in the wage and salary bill.

There is a school of thought in the trade union movement which considers that a firm's ability to pay has no connection with what it ought to pay for a given job. This is a heady concept, but if one examines patterns of wage and salary levels, it becomes very obvious indeed that there is a fine balance between what a company can pay and what it does pay. Nowhere is this relationship more important than in companies who rely on exports for a substantial part of their income.

The allocation of a firm's income to the factors of production has long been of interest to economists. Adam Smith pondered the problem after visiting a pin factory in the eighteenth century, where productivity had increased substantially as a result of job specialization. Karl Marx examined the matter, with typical tedious tenacity, in *Das Kapital*. Those familiar with this work of the Dickensian era will recollect that,

65

according to Marx, capital is the means of producing surplus value. Surplus value is the result of the process of production, and is that part of the value of the product which is not returned – in wages – to the labour force.

Marx argued forcefully that the value of every commodity consists of the labour expended on it, and that this value is measured in terms of the time taken to produce it.

Marx contended that the value of any commodity is determined by its socially necessary costs of production. Labour requires a wage sufficient to maintain a socially acceptable standard of living; commodities are produced in quantities sufficient to meet the social demand. Since this social demand cannot be predicted with any accuracy, he reasoned that the resulting market value of a commodity tends to fluctuate about its theoretical value.

The theory of surplus value dominated the purely economic deductions of *Das Kapital*. It had, and still has, the great advantage of basic truth, since it is unquestionable that the employees of a firm produce more net income for the firm than they themselves receive in wages and salaries. How much more we shall now examine in greater detail than was available to Marx, who wrote in an age when information relating to industry was virtually non-existent.

Most nations nowadays maintain comprehensive statistics regarding industrial output, employment, wages, salaries, and many other factors relevant to their economic well-being. Few nations, however, can match the volume of information which has been compiled in the United States, much of which is available as far back as the early 1800s. It was, of course, in 1886 that the productivity of U.S. manufacturing industry first exceeded that of Britain. Since then the gap has slowly widened, until today the U.S. worker produces about two and a half times the output of his British counterpart, and as far as can be judged, about three times as much as his Russian counterpart.

The passion of the average American for statistics is indicative of the inquiring mind which may well have played a considerable part in establishing the pre-eminence of the U.S.A. as an industrial power. American industry statistics are exceedingly good and very comprehensive. Since they cover a long time span, they can be helpful in assessing trends, and for examining the changes in relationships which historically have occurred during periods of boom or slump.

The primary relationship we shall now examine is the ratio Wages plus Salaries to Added Value. This ratio is indicative of the relationship between Income and Productivity as follows:

(a) $\text{Employee incomes} = \dfrac{\text{Wages} + \text{Salaries}}{\text{Hours Worked}}$

(b) $\text{Employee productivity} = \dfrac{\text{Added Value}}{\text{Hours Worked}}$

(c) $\dfrac{\text{Incomes}}{\text{Productivity}} = \dfrac{\text{Wages} + \text{Salaries}}{\text{Added Value}} = \dfrac{W+S}{A.V.}$

If the ratio $W+S/A.V.$ increases, incomes are rising faster than productivity: if it reduces, the reverse applies. Stable prices can only be achieved in the long term if $W+S/A.V.$ remains constant. (It will be appreciated that salaries (S) are generally classified as a fixed expense, and thus, in the short term, changes in levels of activity can affect the ratio.)

$W+S/A.V.$ also represents the wage and salary cost per unit of output, as well as the employee share of the company's net income. (Added Value is both the net output and the net income.)

Summarizing, it will be evident that the ratio $W+S/A.V.$ represents three different economic aspects of an enterprise, as follows:

1. The relationship between incomes and productivity.
2. The employment cost per unit of output.
3. The employee share of net income.

Each of these three is the same thing, looked at from a different viewpoint, just as national income, national expenditure, and national production are the same thing from a different viewpoint.

Let us now look at this relationship $W+S/A.V.$ for U.S. manufacturing industry from 1889 to 1969, as shown in Figure 9. It is immediately obvious from this that the employees' share of net income is about 50 per cent. In times of boom labour bids up its share, firms raise wages to attract labour, or a combination of both, and the ratio increases. This happened during the period of steady expansion in the U.S.A. between 1900 and 1920, when labour's share increased from 47 per cent to 57 per cent. During the same period, of course, the wage and salary cost per unit of output rose by 21 per cent. Then came the slump, and the process went into reverse for a period of twelve years before the long, slow climb back to prosperity began.

After World War II there was a brief period of boom resulting from the Korean war before the ratio started to revert once again towards 50 per cent. But note the unhealthy trend upwards in the late 1960s.

The figure of 50 per cent is interesting. Karl Marx was of the opinion that workers had to work for half a shift merely to earn their wages. Once their wages had been covered, they worked the other half of the

FIGURE 9: U.S. MANUFACTURING INDUSTRY 1889–1969

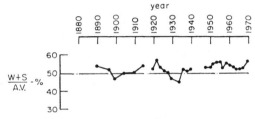

Source: U.N. Statistical Office

shift providing surplus value for the capitalists. Surplus Value is virtually the same as Added Value, but no doubt U.S. industrialists would be horrified to learn that they were conforming to the Marxist theory!

Figure 9 shows U.S. manufacturing industry since 1889. Is this ratio $W+S/A.V.$ equally valid for other countries? The answer would seem that it would be, since the purpose of industry throughout the world is to produce Added Value by converting raw materials into finished goods for consumption or investment. It is the process of conversion which creates Added Value, and it is the labour cost required for this which primarily determines the competitive ability of a country or a firm. Further, since both terms of the ratio are in common units, it is applicable for comparisons between countries, without problems of currency conversion.

In a capitalist economy one would normally expect to see a fairly consistent set of relationships between the incomes of the individual factors of production and the income of a firm. This is because all firms need to pay interest on their capital, and need to increase and renew their capital. They must pay rents for the land they occupy, and

68

they must pay labour for the work done. An increase in the percentage apportioned to one factor of production (say labour) will result in a similar decrease to another (say capital renewal). Generally speaking, since most firms and most nations require returns of similar magnitude for the various factors of production, it follows that roughly the same relationships should apply.

Figure 10 shows labour's share of Added Value for a number of industrial nations for the year 1963. While it will be appreciated that there are differences in the structure of industry between these countries,

FIGURE 10: INTERNATIONAL MANUFACTURING 1963

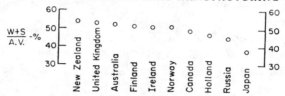

Source: U.N. Statistical Office

and in the method of deriving the statistics, nevertheless it is considered that Figure 10 gives a reasonable indication of labour's share. In the case of Japan it is likely that the ratio is considerably higher in real terms than indicated, since many Japanese employees enjoy fringe benefits, such as housing, education, nursery facilities and holiday hostels, which are supplied by the firms but are not necessarily included in the statistics as wages and salaries. However, even allowing for these fringe benefits, it is unlikely that the true employee share of Added Value in Japanese industry exceeds 45 per cent. This would imply that a high percentage of company income is available for investment in new plant and equipment, which in its turn would suggest a high rate of productivity increase.

Changes in $W+S/A.V.$ over time are indicative of changes in wage and salary costs per unit of output. Suppose that for a given company, this ratio increases from 55 per cent to 60 per cent. This means that 60 per cent of the company's income is paid out in wages and salaries, leaving 40 per cent for other fixed expenses, including rent, rates and cash flow. Now it is likely that the company will require a cash flow* of, let us say, 25 per cent of its net income if it is to pay dividends, replace

* Pre-tax profits plus depreciation.

fixed assets, install new machinery, and provide working capital for expansion. If the cash flow was sufficient to provide the necessary 25 per cent when labour's share was 55 per cent it would obviously reduce to 20 per cent when labour's share increased to 60 per cent, other things being equal. If this 20 per cent was unacceptable to the company for its long-term security, something positive would have to be done to retrieve the situation.

One way in which a company can increase its residual income after paying its employees is to increase labour productivity. Another way is to reduce operating costs, by better use of raw materials and improved process efficiency. A third way is to raise prices, and this in fact is what generally happens when incomes outstrip productivity. It may not happen immediately if the economy is booming, since a company operating at a high level of activity, well above the break-even point, is likely to be making good profits, and may be able to tolerate an increase in labour's share for a certain time. Sooner or later it will have to raise prices if it is unable to generate the required cash flow in any other way.

The effect of a price increase is to reduce labour's share, the amount of reduction depending on the increase. Students of collective bargaining will be familiar with the four points frequently submitted by the unions as the justification for wage claims, namely:

1. The cost of living has gone up.
2. Company profits have increased.
3. Pay differentials have widened.
4. Our members want more money.

Increased prices frequently result in agitation for higher pay. If granted, labour's share increases, causing companies to increase prices. So the merry-go-round goes round, and each time, unless the wage increase is matched by a productivity increase, the value of the currency reduces, and the nation suffers a little more inflation.

Having seen how labour's share varies from country to country (Figure 10) it is perhaps worth examining inflation in these same countries. This is shown in Table 13.

It is quite apparent from the table which country has the most efficient incomes policy!

70

TABLE 13: PRICE INFLATION

Country	Average Rate of Price Increase – % per Annum	
	1955–1970	1960–1965
Japan	1·9	4·2
Finland	5·6	4·1
Ireland	2·2	3·7
Netherlands	1·9	3·3
United Kingdom	2·6	3·0
Norway	2·0	2·9
Australia	2·7	2·1
Canada	2·3	2·0
New Zealand	1·7	1·8
Russia	−1·0	−0·5

Source: Econtel Research Limited

The examination, on an international basis, of labour's share of a company's income is perhaps mainly of interest to economists. Nevertheless, the fact that labour's share is reasonably constant, even in countries with very different social systems, is useful support information to have available when one is considering the eternal question of what is a fair day's pay for a fair day's work.

It would be a bold man indeed who were to claim that he knew the answer to this question, for how does one judge a person's value to the nation? To each according to his work? If so, we must be able to measure equitably the value of work. To each according to his need? If so, there must be a general, acceptable measure of need, and no envy on the part of those who do more work, but have less need and are therefore paid less. Responsibility? Length of Training? Discretionary Authority?

It has been argued that Job Evaluation is a logical and acceptable method of deciding on levels of pay. Admittedly, Job Evaluation can be helpful in making people think about pay in a consistent and logical way, but, unfortunately, all too often it is not logic which is the final arbiter. It is emotion.

Professor Elliott Jaques of Brunel University has developed a method of payment evaluation based on the time span of responsibility. 'Time span' can briefly be defined as the period of time between action and the consequences of that action.

A signalman has great responsibilities, and many lives are in his care. But his time span is only a few minutes, from the moment he pulls

71

levers and otherwise arranges for the transit of a train through his section to the time he hands it over to the next section. If he takes the wrong action, the results will be unpleasantly obvious in a very short time.

At the other end of the scale, the decisions of the chief executive of a large company have a time span of several years. Indeed, most of the actions he initiates are likely to affect the company and its well-being many years ahead, for if he is not concerned with the future rather than the present he is unlikely to be successful.

The Jaques theory has been developed over many years. One is bound to wonder how the theory would evaluate the time span of responsibility of the expert who cut the Cullinan diamond, or the construction men who build New York's skyscrapers. Nevertheless the time span theory has provided a valuable contribution to the analysis of wages and salaries, and has a great deal to commend it.

In the last analysis, in a free society, wages tend to be the result of free bargains between free men. Incomes policies, as applied by eager or desperate Governments, have shown a regrettable tendency to halve the average rate of wage increase for about a year, and to double the rate for the next year, the last state being worse than the first.

In the world of international manufacturing, labour's share of Added Value is generally of the magnitude of 50–55 per cent. Within the United Kingdom the same sort of relationship applies, with the average for the entire United Kingdom manufacturing industry, covering eight million employees, being 50·1 per cent in 1968.

The extraordinary feature of wage bargaining in a free society is that, almost invariably, labour's share depends on labour productivity. This is illustrated in Figure 11, which shows labour's share related to productivity for a number of United Kingdom industries. (Labour's share is, of course, the same as the Wage and Salary Cost per unit of output, or $W+S/A.V.$)

The industries analysed in Figure 11 were as follows:

Cement	Iron and Steel	Radio and Radar
Chemical	Iron Castings	Shipbuilding
Copper and Brass	Man-made Fibres	Textile Finishing
Drop Forgings	Mechanical Engineering	Tractors
Electrical Engineering	Motor Vehicles	Wire and Wire Manufacture
Electrical Machinery	Pottery	

For the above industries productivity, in terms of Added Value per man hour, increased by about 40 per cent between 1963 and 1968. One would thus expect a productivity of £1,000 in 1963 to be £1,400 in 1968, and £2,000 to be £2,800 in 1968. Figure 11 shows that this is virtually what happened, the 1963 line simply moving up the y axis by $1\cdot4\times$ the 1963 values. Also the range of labour's share shifted slightly along the x axis by an amount equal to about 5 per cent of Added Value.

FIGURE 11: PRODUCTIVITY AND UNIT EMPLOYMENT COSTS

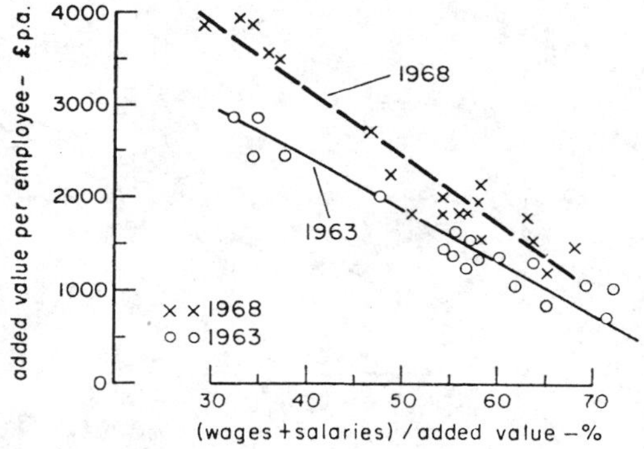

Source: Census of Production.

Figure 11 indicates that the higher the productivity, the lower labour's share. This is exactly what we would expect, since productivity results from capital expenditure on new factories, new machines and new equipment. This additional capital needs to be serviced, and in consequence, more of the company income has to be allotted to the capital factor of production, and less to the labour factor.

Although labour's share decreases with increasing productivity, it by no means follows that the average pay per employee decreases. Quite the reverse, as we see from Figure 12. This shows that pay tends to increase as productivity increases.

For convenience, Figure 11 has been drawn showing a linear relationship, but the exact correlation between the two variables is of secondary importance. What does matter is that all the evidence indicates that there is a positive relationship between productivity and pay in the context of employee remuneration. Companies who, willingly or un-

73

willingly, pay more than is justified by their level of productivity are likely to find their competitive ability seriously endangered.

In the practical world of modern industry, the facts indicate that rates of pay *are* conditioned by what a company can afford. Let it stray either side of a fairly narrow band of wage levels, and the company may well find itself in difficulty. If it is successful, and is paying less than it can afford, it will be faced with wage claims, or it will itself raise wages to

FIGURE 12: PRODUCTIVITY AND PAY

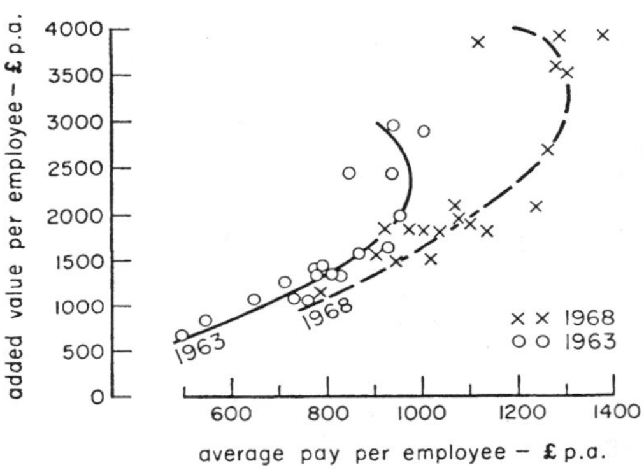

average pay per employee − £ p.a.

Source: Census of Production, H.M.S.O.

obtain labour, thus increasing rates to conform to the industry norm. If it is paying more than it can afford, then it will indeed be in trouble, with low or non-existent profit margins, and possibly hoping, like Mr Micawber, for something to turn up.

Labour's share of the net income of an enterprise is not just a topic for academic theorists. It is a subject of great practical importance, and every company has much to gain by maintaining careful records relating to changes in this share, and to changes in the share of the other factors of production, over time. By relating labour's share to labour productivity a company can predict, with considerable accuracy, the rates it can afford to pay. It may not be able to answer the perennial question of what is a fair wage, but is not a fair wage that which is a just and reasonable share of the net income of the enterprise?

74

Chapter 8

The Productivity of Capital

In the last analysis, a company is in business to make a profit. Profit is the final output, and in a capitalist society there is no future for the private enterprise company which always makes a loss.

Profit is essential, but it would be wrong to assume that every action initiated by a Board of Directors is aimed at maximizing profits, irrespective of social consequences. This assumption has frequently been accepted without qualification by those who have only an inadequate knowledge of company affairs, and whose opinions are more easily expressed in clear divisions of black and white than in the subtler and more accurate shades of grey. For example, many companies support local charities, run expensive welfare schemes, and help their old-age pensioners, in obvious breach of the dogma that every action is aimed at improving the absolute level of profit. Admittedly, the cynics would say that a company only does good deeds so that its work-people will think what a splendid firm it is, and be prepared to work for less money, or to go on strike less frequently, thus indirectly helping to maximize profits. The true cynic, of course, is always able to find a devious ulterior motive for anything and everything, in spite of well-substantiated evidence to the contrary.

That there are firms who would always act to maximize profits, irrespective of human suffering, is unquestionable. It is equally unquestionable that many firms do, honestly and sincerely, attempt to honour the principles of the Marlow Declaration, even if by so doing they benefit their employees at the expense of their shareholders.

It is unfortunate that, in the United Kingdom at least, the word 'profit' is almost looked upon as a term of abuse. For that matter, so is the word 'capitalist', which conjures up the image of a well-fed gentleman climbing into a Rolls-Royce across the prostrate bodies of his exploited workers.

The English language has many words which provoke the emotions. Rabble rousers throughout the ages have traded on the propensity of people to lose all sense of proportion when their passions are inflamed. The man who is rational and even-tempered as an individual is capable of becoming completely oblivious to reason when part of a crowd; in such circumstances he is an easy target for the militant orator, who well knows how to sway the masses with a few well-chosen words.

A popular technique of the rabble rouser is to suggest that his listeners are being cheated of what is rightly theirs. This rarely fails, since most people are convinced, in their heart of hearts, that the whole social system would be vastly improved if there were more like them. From this ego-satisfying conceit it naturally follows that society does not recognize their worth. Since the purse strings of society are held by the capitalists, it is immediately evident to followers of this logic that the profits of the capitalists should be distributed to those who produce it – the workers – and not to those who do nothing other than subscribe money to the enterprise – the shareholders.

Whatever one's views may be on the morality of profit, it is a fact that the capital stock of the community can only increase as a result of profit. In its simplest sense, profit may be defined as the difference between total income and total expense over a period of time. Without profit, and its offspring capital investment, no company can hope to survive.

Profit is the ultimate output of a firm. We might therefore measure the efficiency of a company in terms of the profit resulting from the combination of the two main factors of production, namely labour and capital. One way of doing this would be to use the ratios Profit per Employee and Profit : Capital Employed as key operating statistics for the company.

There is scant evidence to suggest that many firms pay much attention to the profit earned per employee. This is perfectly understandable, since everyone knows that profit per employee can vary widely for reasons quite unconnected with managerial efficiency. However, firms are rarely inattentive to the relationship between Profit and Capital Employed.

If one were to ask senior executives to state the two most important criteria for assessing company profitability, it is almost certain that

76

most of them would quote Profit : Sales, and Profit : Capital Employed. In all probability, it would be pointed out that:

$$\frac{\text{Profit}}{\text{Capital Employed}} = \frac{\text{Profit}}{\text{Sales}} \times \frac{\text{Sales}}{\text{Capital Employed}}$$

There is wide acceptance of Profit : Capital Employed as the measure of profitability. For example, the comment was made in *The Times 1000** that '. . . the most profitable firms, measured by their returns on capital employed, are rarely to be found among the biggest companies.' However, the serious disadvantage of this ratio is that it is of little use for measuring company performance other than over a period of years.

It would be utterly ridiculous to suggest that return on capital is not an important criterion. To achieve long-term stability and growth, it is essential that a firm maintains and, if possible, increases its stock of capital. Indeed, without such an increase it is unlikely that it will be able to improve labour productivity, which is so necessary for the control of unit wage costs. How then does a firm increase its stock of capital? The answer is, 'by ploughing back retained profits', or 'by raising money through a share issue or other similar flotation'. Both of these methods are only feasible if the company earns a consistently good profit on its capital employed. The investing public expects a certain return on the capital it supplies to industry, and if company A cannot produce the required return, and company B can, then company B will attract the money.

Return on capital is important for defining the absolute profit one requires from a given level of assets. However, when we are considering the month by month operations of a company, we must endeavour to relate the capital employed not to profit, but to company output, that is, to Added Value. In other words, we must try to measure the productivity of capital.

The great difficulty in any discussion concerning capital is to define how one values it. Is fixed capital at book value? At original value? At replacement value? And then there is the matter of stocks. Do these consist of raw materials, work in progress, or finished goods?

All the best accountants can argue happily for hours about the subtler distinctions between fixed assets and current assets, and how they should

* Published by Times Newspapers, 1970.

77

be valued. For the purposes of interfirm comparisons these distinctions do matter. Within a given firm, however, they do not really affect the situation, provided that the assets are valued on a consistent basis, and that fluctuating rates of depreciation are not applied. As with all matters relating to the measurement of performance, consistency over time is the essential feature.

We have mentioned that, for reasons of control, we must try to measure the productivity of capital. The sceptic may well ask whether this can serve any useful purpose, particularly in view of the discrepancies which can arise due to methods of capital valuation. A possible reply to this question would be to point out that the overall efficiency of a company results from the combination of a large number of diverse factors. No single factor can be examined in isolation from the others, and one must examine all relevant items, using the most suitable measures available. Having decided on a measure, we must standardize on it. Having agreed on certain procedures for the valuation and depreciation of capital, these must be applied consistently.

This is particularly true if one is looking at either labour or capital productivity. Irrespective of the method adopted for measurement, the absolute level of labour productivity tends to be conditioned by the productivity of capital. If we adopt Added Value as a measure of output, we find that as the Added Value per Employee (or Labour Productivity) increases, the Added Value per £1 of capital tends to decrease. This is illustrated in Figure 13, which is based on a survey carried out in 1968 by Urwick, Orr and Partners Limited across a number of firms in the engineering industry.

If we attempt to assess the relative efficiency of firms A and B in Figure 13 it is immediately apparent that A is the more efficient, since A produces more output per unit of labour input than B, for similar capital productivity. Again, D is more efficient than C since D produces more output per unit of capital than C, for similar labour productivity.

It is easy to relate C's efficiency to D's, and A's to B's, but the problem becomes more complex if we try to compare A with D. In this case the answer is not so obvious. One way of assessment would be to evaluate labour in terms of capital. For this to be meaningful, many factors would have to be considered, such as rates of pay, investment grants, regional employment premiums, and so on. Labour would have a different equivalent capital value in different parts of the country, but

78

undoubtedly one could produce a fair approximation of this value if necessary.

In practice, for purposes of company control, it is rarely necessary to do this exercise. It is necessary to be aware of the general relationship between resource inputs, but having said this one is more interested in measuring improvements against given criteria than in evolving complex theories for reducing all resources to one common denominator.

Industry has two primary resources, namely labour and capital. The productivity of labour determines the standard of living of the nation, but the productivity of capital determines whether it will be able to

FIGURE 13: LABOUR CAPITAL PRODUCTIVITY

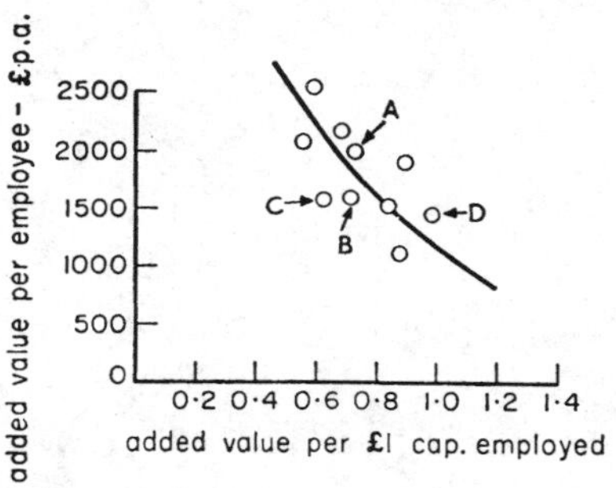

attract the investment which sooner or later will be required if economic growth is to be maintained.

Let us accept that, for all its limitations as a short term criterion of performance, the ratio Profit : Capital Employed is the ultimate measure of managerial effectiveness. It is difficult to be specific about the definition of a satisfactory return on capital. Jacques Servan-Schreiber comments that net profits should be 12 to 13 per cent of equity capital in order to maintain growth in areas of advanced technology. In surveys concerning profitability, the majority of medium sized companies in the United Kingdom, employing some 250–750 people, have stated that their target is 20 per cent pre-tax profit to capital employed. Larger companies, who find it easier to raise additional capital, tend to aim for 15 per cent. For example, the Chairman of Britain's largest international engineering group, G.K.N. Limited, stated in his annual report to the shareholders that the results for the year 1969 had fulfilled expectations. He continued: 'But for the effect of the revaluation of assets in John Lysaght (Australia) Limited, the return on net assets would have been 13.9 per cent, thus bringing us within attainable distance of our established 15 per cent target.'

If we examine the performance of companies, in terms of Profit : Capital Employed, it is apparent that a target of 15 per cent before tax and interest is not unrealistic in terms of what is actually being achieved. Some typical company results are quoted in Table 14, for both the private and nationalized sectors of industry.

TABLE 14: RETURN ON CAPITAL EMPLOYED

Company	Turnover	Pre-Tax Profit: Capital Employed*
Private Sector	£ p.a.	%
Dunlop	450 m.	14·2
Hawker Siddeley	382 m.	9·2
Rolls-Royce	320 m.	13·2
Sears Holdings	266 m.	13·6
Tube Investments	250 m.	8·3
Joseph Lucas	213 m.	19·9
Blackwood Hodge	44 m.	18·1
Sheepbridge Engineering	17 m.	14·1
Hawtin Industries	16 m.	22·1
Nationalized Sector		
National Coal Board		4·4
Gas Industry Area Boards		4·5
British European Airways		4·1
British Overseas Airways Corp.		15·9

* Total tangible assets less current liabilities and sundry provisions.
Source: The Times 500, 1969–70

In 1969–70 the average return on capital employed of the five hundred largest firms in the United Kingdom was 17·10 per cent. It must be reiterated that profit is a residual, and is greatly affected by changes in levels of output. Capital employed can vary depending on the accounting convention in use, on whether machinery and buildings are owned outright or leased, on the valuation of fixed assets, and on such matters as raw material costs, where price increases can easily result in a profit bonus through an increase in stock valuation. In spite of these and other factors affecting profit and capital, it still would appear to be a valid proposition that the 15 per cent Profit : Capital Employed ratio is reasonably typical for British industry.

When comparing the performance of a number of companies, be it for investment, takeover or general appraisal purposes, the return on capital is a useful yardstick. The proviso is that trends must be examined over several years. In the shorter term, we can obtain a much more helpful assessment of the effective use of capital by looking at the relationship between different types of asset and the output resulting from these. In other words, by examining the relationship between Assets and Added Value.

The starting point for assessing capital productivity is the ratio Profit : Capital Employed. This ratio is the product of Profit : Sales and Sales : Capital Employed. Since Sales Value does not represent the net output, and is not a measure of the work done in the production of goods or services, it is preferable to express the profitability of capital as follows:

$$\frac{\text{Profit}}{\text{Capital Employed}} = \frac{\text{Profit}}{\text{Added Value}} \times \frac{\text{Added Value}}{\text{Capital Employed}}$$

The importance of the two terms on the right-hand side of the equation cannot be over-emphasized; both must be maximized in order to maximize Profit : Capital Employed.

The first charge on the income of a company is the payment of the employees. Thus a company must constantly examine the percentage of its Added Value paid out in wages and salaries. Having paid the employees, it then must allocate a further percentage of Added Value to the remaining fixed expenses of the company. Finally, whatever it has left will be available for profit – hence the significance of the ratio Profit : Added Value. The ratio Added Value : Capital Employed represents the productivity of capital.

The capital employed by a company can be subdivided into Fixed Assets and Working Capital. In turn, these can be broken down further, typically* as follows:

Fixed Assets:

Land+Buildings+Machinery

Working Capital:

Current Assets—Current Liabilities =
    (Stocks+Debtors+Cash)—(Creditors+Other Liabilities)

* Trade investments are generally included in Fixed Assets. For simplicity we shall neglect this item.

If we now invert the term Added Value/Capital Employed, we can equate it to its two main constituents as follows:

$$\frac{\text{Capital Employed}}{\text{Added Value}} = \frac{\text{Fixed Assets}}{\text{Added Value}} + \frac{\text{Working Capital}}{\text{Added Value}}$$

From this equation we can develop a comprehensive ratio chart, itemized down to the last nut and bolt if necessary. An actual chart might appear as follows, looking rather like a family tree with all the branches leading to the ultimate objective of Profit/Capital Employed.

CHART A: GENERAL RATIOS

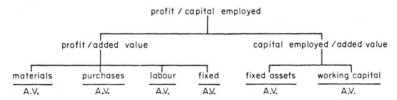

The senior management of a company rarely needs to study a more detailed breakdown than that shown. Most people would agree that too much information is as unhelpful as too little. The brain quickly becomes confused when confronted with masses of information, and every successful manager knows that the hallmarks of an effective information system are brevity and objectivity.

There are circumstances where it can be advantageous to subdivide the chart further than shown above – for example, when comparing performance between different companies within a large group. On the capital side, a further breakdown could be undertaken as follows:

CHART B: CAPITAL PRODUCTIVITY RATIOS

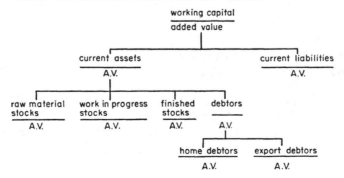

With a little imagination one could go on happily breaking down elements of cost until one covered several pages. By this time the object of the exercise would probably be lost.

In the field of company control, information, to be effective, must readily indicate trends and changes in trend. It must enable those in authority to locate areas of incipient trouble, and to take action where action is required.

Charts A and B show how a given objective, in this case Profit : Capital Employed, can be divided and subdivided into a number of ratios, each ratio expressing a stated resource input in terms of output (i.e. Added Value). By an examination of trends over time, those inputs which are resulting in a greater or less output can be readily identified. To illustrate this, we will look at the productivity ratios applying to a well-established engineering firm near Birmingham, England. This firm, Wrogerson and Co. Limited, employs some 350 people, and has an annual turnover of £2,000,000. The company's business is fabricating steel.

The figures in the following example are based on fact, but, for obvious reasons, the name of the firm is fictitious. The ratios quoted relate to the first six months of 1970. It is company practice for these to be presented for the consideration of the Board at the Director's Monthly Meeting, held on the third Monday of each month.

Table 15 shows the layout of the form itemizing the General Ratios, and Table 16 the layout of the Capital Productivity Form. The actual figures for the months under review have been inserted, and from these we can see the changes which occurred over six months. It is perhaps worth mentioning that, whenever Added Value is the denominator, the smaller the ratio the better the profitability.

TABLE 15: WROGERSON LIMITED, GENERAL RATIOS, PERIODS 1 AND 2, 1970

	Objective Ratios	% Per Annum					
		Jan.	Feb.	Mar.	Apr.	May	June
Profit: Capital Employed	15·0	13·4	10·4	11·3	11·3	11.0	11·4
Profit: Added Value	27·6	25·0	20·5	21·7	21·2	21·4	21·8
Materials: A.V.	171·0	179·0	186·0	183·0	184·0	179·0	178·0
Purchases: A.V.	30·5	30·0	32·0	32·3	32·5	32·5	31·9
Production Labour: A.V.	31·0	34·2	34·4	34·1	33·6	34·0	34·1
Fixed: A.V.	41·4	40·8	45·1	44·2	45·2	44·6	44·1
Capital Employed: Added Value	184·0	185·0	198·0	192·0	188·0	194·0	192·0
Fixed Assets: A.V.	72·0	75·0	82·0	82·0	80·0	76·0	75·0
Working Capital: A.V.	112·0	110·0	116·0	110·0	108·0	118·0	117·0

TABLE 16: WROGERSON LIMITED, CAPITAL PRODUCTIVITY,
PERIODS 1 AND 2, 1970

% *Per Annum*

	Objective Ratios	Jan.	Feb.	Mar.	Apr.	May	June
Current Assets: A.V.	138·0	136·0	142·0	133·0	131·0	137·0	138·0
Raw Material Stocks: A.V.	33·5	36·8	35·0	29·0	26·4	27·0	27·0
Work In Progress: A.V.	9·0	8·0	9·5	9·0	8·4	7·0	7·2
Finished: A.V.	11·2	9·2	12·5	13·0	9·2	15·0	11·8
Debtors: A.V.	84·3	82·0	85·0	82·0	87·0	88·0	92·0
Current Liabilities: A.V.	26·0	26·0	26·0	23·0	23·0	19·0	21·0

When examining Tables 15 and 16 it is useful to recall that the following relationships apply:

Added Value = Production Labour+Fixed+Profit.

Working Capital = Current Assets−Current Liabilities.

The column headed 'Objective Ratios' was prepared as the standards of performance which must be achieved to reach the objective profit of 15 per cent Return on Capital, at the budget level of sales and capital employed.

If information is to be useful in management control, it must be so presented as to highlight areas of potential change or trouble. This should be sufficient to trigger off the necessary action by those in authority. As the philosopher Edmund Burke remarked, when he was asked whether it was a good thing that the American colonies had unilaterally declared their independence of Britain, 'The question is not so much whether it is a good thing or a bad thing, but what you are going to do about it that matters.'

The diagnosis of a company's areas of inefficiency is relatively simple. It is the cure that is difficult. Yet in spite of the techniques of diagnosis which have been developed in recent years, there is evidence that many firms do not find it easy to know where they are going wrong. In support of this statement, *Business Ratios** once published a survey which analysed the performance of 100 companies which went bankrupt in 1965. Whilst it was admitted that luck was not on the side of these companies (as Napoleon's generals would have claimed on their own behalf), it was also concluded that over 70 per cent of the companies were mismanaged, and that they were unaware of impending failure.

*A Dun and Bradstreet publication.

It is a matter of history that the report of the Official Receiver also commented that the bankrupt companies in the survey had been mismanaged. 'Indifferent book-keeping, managerial extravagance, and Micawber-like optimism all contributed to disaster.' In spite of these shortcomings, the Receiver suggested that all might still have been well if the companies had bothered to set up effective control systems. The moral is obvious.

The efficiency with which a company utilizes its resources is a matter of fundamental importance not only to the company and its employees, but also to society at large. Efficient management, as responsible economists are wont to say, does not guarantee the achievement of social objectives. In spite of this, it is undoubtedly true that the more efficient the management, the greater will be the Added Value produced by individual firms in the economy and the higher the gross Domestic Product.

What makes an efficient manager has been a problem to which no complete answer has yet been found. Are managers born or made? Do knowledge and discipline produce wisdom and humanity? How does one learn the art of handling people? These questions and many similar are of extreme relevance to behavioural scientists and industrialists in the 1970s, in a period when industry is looking anew at its social obligations.

Whatever the answers may be, one thing is certain. No chief executive, or Board of Directors, can be fully effective without having a thorough awareness of what is to be achieved. The desired achievement may be expressed in a number of ways such as Profit : Capital Employed, Absolute Profit, Profit : Sales, or Sales : Capital Employed. However he judges achievement, the truly professional manager is always aware that his job consists of allocating resources, making decisions, and working through other people. Management begins with man, and no matter how sophisticated the techniques which may be used for the management of capital, these will be of little avail if the human side is neglected.

Chapter 9

Costing and Cost Standards

Plautus is reputed to have said, nearly two thousand years ago when Rome was in the high summer of her power, 'There cannot any profit remain if the costs exceed it.' A wise comment in any period of history!

In order to make a profit, a company must sell its products at a price which will more than cover the costs of production. Over a period of time, the revenue resulting from sales must be greater than total expenses if profit is to result. Under normal conditions of trading, a company aims to price its products in relation to cost. There are instances where this is not so, but they are unusual.

A classic example of selling a product at a price unrelated to production costs is that of the early steam engines made by Boulton and Watt at the Soho Manufactory in Birmingham. Contrary to popular belief, James Watt did not invent the steam engine. His great achievement was to improve their efficiency. Watt's engines were so efficient, in comparison with others of the age, that his colleague, the archetypal entrepreneur Matthew Boulton, decided that they should not be sold for a fixed price. Rather, the purchaser should pay Boulton and Watt a sum of money equal to $33\frac{1}{3}$ per cent of the cost savings made possible by the wonder engines, such payments continuing until expiration of the patents.

This interesting arrangement worked reasonably well, since the savings were substantial. As may be expected, however, problems were encountered, since the purchasers tended to pay when business was good, and to plead inability when times were bad. Also, there were frequent arguments about the actual savings which had accrued, since the costing procedures of the eighteenth century were somewhat lacking in sophistication. Yet in spite of all difficulties, there is little doubt that both parties to the bargain benefited, and it was not until later years that the

86

engines were sold at a quoted price. By the time this happened it was Boulton's proud boast that he knew the cost of every engine produced at the Soho Manufactory.

There are parallels today of the system used by Boulton for creating revenue from the sale of engines, particularly in the field of office equipment or special purpose machinery. However, in the vast majority of cases, companies sell their products in the market at prices which are a function of the costs of production. At least, prices are intended to be a function of the costs of production, the problem here being that it is extremely difficult to obtain a true cost. Costs have of necessity to be based on a number of assumptions, and the validity of any cost is no greater than the validity of its constituent assumptions.

Some years ago, Rootes* announced that it was reducing the price of the luxury Humber Snipe saloon by a substantial amount – well over £100. The object was to stimulate sales, and thus to reduce total costs by spreading the fixed expenses associated with the Snipe over a larger number of units. A cost reduction of this nature is, of course, a perfectly legitimate ploy, which relies for success on the generation of substantially increased sales.

The reaction of many people to the Rootes announcement was a sad example of the public's lack of awareness of the relationship between costs, prices and volume of sales. It was too readily assumed, often by those who should have known better, that Rootes must have been making a considerable profit – well over £100 per car – if they could afford to reduce prices by such an amount. In truth, Rootes were very far from making a considerable profit on the Snipe. They were not making a profit at all, and since an increase in sales for this car did not materialize, its production was discontinued.

In the early days of the automobile industry, unit costs were calculated in a simple but effective way. Firstly, the total operating expenses of the factory were added up. Secondly, the number of cars sold was added up. The cost per automobile was then obtained by dividing the number of cars into the total expenditure. This was a splendid way of calculating what the cost per car *had* been over a given period. It was not quite so splendid when the same principle was applied for estimating what the cost per car *would* be in the future. Without such an estimate, how could one prepare a selling price?

* Now Chrysler-U.K.

A particular problem in estimating was to decide the number of cars which would be made in expectation of sales. Operating expenses could generally be forecast with reasonable accuracy. Without similar accuracy in predicting the volume of sales, unit costs could vary considerably between estimate and reality. A company which achieved its forecast sales was very profitable; a company which did not was, in many cases literally, ruined.

The calculation of unit costs by dividing output into total expenses may have been quite acceptable to Henry Ford when costing the Model T. The method is quite useless for companies with a varied product range, all of whom require a much more advanced costing system if they are to be able to measure performance, and to price their products effectively. A factory costing system has three main objects:

1. To allocate expenses, as fairly as possible, to all products presently being made, and hence to enable product costs to be calculated, and budgets to be prepared.

2. To assist management in its control of the factory by measuring actual costs against a given standard.

3. To estimate the cost of all products likely to be made in the future, so that prices may be prepared for quotation purposes.

To understand the principles of costing it is necessary to appreciate that costs are customarily classified as fixed or variable. Admittedly, certain costs are partly fixed and partly variable, and, apart from obvious exceptions such as raw materials and carriage outwards, it is never easy to decide on whether a cost is fixed or variable. Production labour, for example, has traditionally been considered a variable expense, presumably on the principle that labour can be fired when there is a shortage of work, and hired again when business improves. Nevertheless examination of the manning of a number of factories which have experienced a recession indicates very clearly that production labour is not a variable expense. If output falls by 20 per cent, production labour will not show a similar reduction. More likely, it will reduce by about half this amount, or some 10 per cent. Instances could even be quoted of factories who have continued to employ skilled female labour during a recession, paying the women for doing nothing rather than lose them and be unable to have their skills available when trade picked up.

88

Staff salaries are generally classified as a fixed expense, but again it is apparent that this is not so in practice. Numbers of staff do increase as output increases, although not in proportion.

The fact that Production Labour is not a wholly variable cost, and Staff Salaries are not wholly fixed is one reason why the productivity of a company is likely to increase rapidly when levels of output rise. As with a company, so with a nation's productivity. The much publicized productivity increases of 1968 were more a reflection of an upsurge in trade than of improvements in manning standards.

While one can argue endlessly about whether a cost should be classified in one way or another, no effective costing system can be set up without a decision being made as to which expenses are to be considered fixed, and which variable. Part fixed/part variable costs must be apportioned to their constituent elements. For example, if it is decided that the labour involved in plant maintenance is part fixed, part variable, management must decide on the proportion to be allocated to each. If it is decided that a 60 : 40 split is most sensible, then the accountants will allocate 60 per cent of plant maintenance labour to fixed expenses, and 40 per cent to variable. If electric power for factory lighting is 30 per cent fixed, 70 per cent variable, then this item will be apportioned accordingly.

The definition of a fixed cost is one which tends *not* to vary with changing levels of factory output. A variable cost is one which *does* tend to vary with changing levels of output. The object of defining all costs in terms of fixed or variable expense is to enable contribution rates to be calculated, break-even sales to be established, and profit forecasts to be prepared at different levels of output.

The contribution, or, more fully, 'contribution to fixed expenses', is that sum of money which remains when the variable costs of production are deducted from the sales revenue.

Contribution = Sales−Variable costs.

= Fixed Costs+Profit.

Introducing Added Value into the equation we have:

Contribution = Added Value−Production Labour.

It is perhaps easier to understand the various cost relationships by looking at an actual example. If we write down the 1970 objective results for Wrogerson & Co.,* we have the following:

*See Chapter 8, pages 83–4.

TABLE 17: WROGERSON & CO., OBJECTIVE PROFIT, 1970

Budget Year 1970

Objective per Month (*20 days*)

	£	%
Sales	180,000	100·0
Raw Materials	102,000	56·5
	78,000	43·5
Purchases	18,200	10·1
Added Value	59,800	33·4
Production Labour	18,600	10·3
Contribution	41,200	23·1
Fixed Expenses	24,700	13·7
Profit	16,500	9·4

From Table 17 we can calculate the level of sales at which Wrogerson will break even, that is, the level at which the company makes neither a profit nor a loss. The company will break even when the contribution to fixed expenses is exactly equal to the fixed expenses. The contribution is 23·1 per cent of sales. Thus the sales needed to produce a contribution equal to the fixed expenses of £24,700 is £24,700/23·1 × 100, or £107,000. Above this level, profits will accrue at the rate of £23·1 for every £100 additional sales.

Wrogerson classify their main elements of cost as follows:

Materials, bought-out parts, out-work	*Variable*
Plant maintenance, tools, packing, carriage out	*Variable*
Process heat and power	*Variable*
Heat, light, water	*50% Variable*
Production labour, direct and indirect	*Variable*
Staff salaries	*Fixed*
Building maintenance, printing and stationery	*Fixed*
Rent, rates and depreciation	*Fixed*
Heat, light, water	*50% Fixed*

The above classification was only decided and agreed after considerable discussion. Having reached agreement, standard classifications

90

were prepared, and adopted by the accounts department. In this way the company ensured the consistent treatment of expenses over time.

The calculation of product costs in a factory producing a wide range of articles is not easy. Certain costs can readily be obtained – assuming always that proper recording systems are in use. These costs typically relate to raw material usage, production labour, carriage outwards, sub-contract work, and other similar expenses which can be allocated with a fair degree of certainty to a given product. In total, they may well amount to 50 per cent or more of the total product cost.

The allocation of the remaining items of cost to a given product is a matter concerning which many learned books have been written. Suffice it to say that the ultimate ambition of every cost accountant is to allocate every penny of expense to one product or another, using a number of assumptions to decide which product takes what share of a given expense. To assist him in this exercise he will probably divide the factory into cost centres. A cost centre is a section within a factory where costs are collected as though the section was a separate operating unit. Usually a cost centre is an area where one particular process is carried out, and it is likely to be equipped with machines of generally similar value. For example, a light engineering factory producing machined castings might be divided into five cost centres as follows:

1. Foundry
2. Drills.
3. Centre lathes.
4. Milling machines.
5. Despatch warehouse.

Ideally, a cost centre should also be a centre of responsibility, with one particular individual accountable for the successful operation of the whole centre.

The allocation of costs is an exercise which relies on certain assumptions. How should one allocate rent to a given product? If one assumes that rent is proportional to floor area, and a given cost centre represents 10 per cent of factory floor area, it would perhaps not be unreasonable to assume that the cost centre should bear 10 per cent of the rent payable by the company.

What about staff salaries? Or stationery? Or postage and telephones?

91

A decision must be made regarding the allocation of these and other elements of cost, so that the total expenses charged against all cost centres equals the total operating cost of the factory.

It has already been stated that one of the main objects of a costing system is to enable total product costs to be calculated. Total cost may be expressed as follows:

Total Cost = Variable Costs + Fixed Costs.
$\qquad$ = Materials + Purchases + Production Labour + Fixed.

By definition, variable expenses tend to vary with changing levels of output. Thus, the underlying assumption behind the classification of a particular element of cost as a variable expense is that the element cost per unit of output is the same whether 5,000 items are made or 50,000.

As regards fixed expenses, these tend *not* to vary with output. Thus fixed expenses cannot be allocated to a product without first specifying the quantity of the product which is to be made, or which has been made. If the fixed expenses amount to 100p per unit when 5,000 articles are made, they will be 10p per unit when 50,000 are made.

There is no such thing as a total cost for a product unless it is specifically related to quantity. One of the paradoxes of industrial life is that unit costs are at their lowest when a company is operating at a high level of activity, and at their highest when the company is short of work. A company is best able to reduce prices when it is very busy, but will wish to increase them when it is in a recession. Unfortunately for the purely economic approach, quite the reverse applies in practice. Companies tend to raise their prices when they are very busy, in accordance with the old railway adage of charging what the market will stand, and reduce them when they need work, to try and attract extra business.

The problem of fixed expenses allocation has always existed, and is always likely to exist when one wishes to estimate a total cost. It should always be remembered that a total cost is only valid for one particular level of output. Change that level, and the cost will change.

Absorption costing is the term given to the system whereby all fixed and variable costs are charged to a product or a cost centre. It is referred to by this name because it is implicit in the system that every cost has to be absorbed by being allocated to one product or another.

In other words, the factory costs are equal to the number of products produced multiplied by the average cost per product.

In view of the arguments which frequently arise regarding fixed expense allocation, an alternative method of costing has become increasingly popular over the years, particularly in the United States. This method is known as *marginal costing*. In marginal costing only the variable items of expense are charged to a given product, the fixed expenses being ignored. Marginal costing is a powerful tool of management, and the emphasis it places on variable costs has particularly relevance for pricing and for company control.

The theory behind marginal costing is that a factory must incur certain fixed expenses as long as it remains in business. These fixed expenses have to be paid for, and only when this is done will the company make a profit. Every product must be priced so that it will make at least some contribution to fixed expenses, and it is the rate of contribution resulting from the sale of a given product which provides a useful measure of profitability.

Marginal costing and absorption costing do not necessarily provide a similar assessment of product profitability. An example of this statement is given in Table 18, where the costs and margins for three different products are itemized.

TABLE 18: PRODUCT SALES AND REVENUE, JANUARY–MARCH 1970

	Product			
	A	B	C	Total
Sales revenue	100,000	50,000	10,000	160,000
Raw materials	56,000	26,000	4,600	86,600
	44,000	24,000	5,400	73,400
Purchases	10,000	6,000	1,400	17,400
Added Value	34,000	18,000	4,000	56,000
Production labour	11,000	4,000	3,000	18,000
Contribution	23,000	14,000	1,000	38,000
Fixed	18,000	11,000	1,500	30,500
Profit	5,000	3,000	−500	7,500

If we now examine the profitability of these three products, in terms of absorption costing and marginal costing, we have:

TABLE 19: ABSORPTION AND MARGINAL COSTING

Absorption			January–March 1970	
	A	B	C	Total
	£	£	£	£
Sales revenue	100,000	50,000	10,000	160,000
Total costs	95,000	47,000	10,500	152,500
Profit	5,000	3,000	− 500	7,500

Marginal				
	A	B	C	Total
Sales revenue	100,000	50,000	10,000	160,000
Variable costs	77,000	36,000	9,000	122,000
Contribution	23,000	14,000	1,000	38,000
Fixed				30,500
Profit				7,500

Marginal (Products A and B only)			
	A	B	Total
Sales revenue	100,000	50,000	150,000
Variable costs	77,000	36,000	113,000
Contribution	23,000	14,000	37,000
Fixed			30,500
Profit			6,500

With the absorption costing approach, it is evident that product C is losing money, at the rate of £500 per quarter, or £2,000 year. It might therefore be concluded that the company would save £2,000 per year by discontinuing production of C.

If we now look at the marginal costs, it is apparent that C is producing a contribution to fixed expenses at the rate of £1,000 per quarter, or £4,000 per year. On this basis, therefore, since the fixed expenses will be the same whether C is discontinued or not, the company will be £4,000 better off by continuing to produce C.

In this example it is assumed that, if the company stops making C, it will not be able to replace it with another product, nor will this action alter the sales of A and B. Under such circumstances, therefore, there can be no question but that the company should continue to make C. C is making a contribution to fixed expenses, albeit a small one, and this would be lost if the product were to be withdrawn.

This simple example shows that different methods of costing can result in different conclusions.

Accurate cost information is essential for assessing the profitability of a company's product range, and for pricing. In addition, it is virtually essential for the effective control of the day-to-day operations of a business.

Cost control, in common with all systems of control, consists of the comparison of actual results against a criterion. The criterion may be based on historical costs, expected costs, or ideal costs. *Historical* cost standards are set by reference to past achievements. *Expected* cost standards are derived partly from past achievement, and partly from forecasts of cost increases and cost reductions likely in the future. *Ideal* cost standards assume perfect operating conditions, in a perfect world where such nuisances as machine breakdowns, idle time through bad planning, and other stoppages do not exist. It will be appreciated that ideal cost standards are generally quite unrealistic, and hence of little practical use for control purposes.

Historical cost standards have the great virtue, provided the recording systems for job times, material usage, and manning standards are adequate, of indicating what has been achieved in the past. They are therefore realistic, and for this reason are more likely to be accepted by the line managers responsible for cost centre production costs. Acceptability is a prerequisite of a successful control system, for it must always be remembered that those whose responsibility it is to set up management information systems are rarely those who are accountable for the operating results.

The disadvantage of a historical standard is that things change. Raw material costs can go up or down. Rates of pay can fluctuate, although they generally show a strong upward trend, particularly at the end of a period of wage restraint. Electricity and fuel costs may alter, and indeed most items of cost do not remain the same from one year to the next.

Expected cost standards are probably the most suitable for the majority of companies, combining as they do the realism of historical costs, with the adjustments which are necessary if forecast cost changes are to be incorporated in the standard.

However the standard is set, a standard costing system will provide management with a comparison between actual and standard costs. The amount by which one differs from the other is called a variance, and an analysis of the variances is an essential feature of the system.

95

The philosophy underlying variances is that the standard cost, plus or minus the variance (whichever is the case), is equal to the actual cost.

A simple but effective standard costing system, introduced by an engineering company near Coventry employing 180 people, uses continually up-dated historical cost standards, against which the actual costs are compared. After the necessary adjustments have been made to raw material and conversion costs, to compensate for changes in stock levels, the trading statement is issued, typically as in Table 20.

TABLE 20: TRADING STATEMENT – STANDARD COST PRESENTATION

	Actual		Standard		Variance £	
	£	%	£	%	Over	Under
Sales	56,000	100·0	56,000	100·0		
Materials	29,000	52·0	28,800	51·5	200	—
	27,000	48·0	27,200	48·5		
Purchases	6,800	12·2	6,700	12·0	100	—
Added Value	20,200	35·8	20,500	36·5		—
Prod. labour	7,200	12·7	6,800	12·1	400	—
Contribution	13,000	23·1	13,700	24·4		
Fixed	8,900	15·9	8,800	15·6	100	—
Profit	4,100	7·2	4,900	8·8	800	—

The standards in Table 20 were derived by taking a four-month moving average for the ratios Material : Sales, Purchases : Sales, Added Value : Sales, and Labour : Added Value. These ratios were then applied to the actual sales, and a standard contribution obtained. From this contribution the expected fixed expenses were deducted, to give a standard profit.

An effective control system should clearly indicate the areas where action in necessary. Unless it does this, then it can be stated with complete certainty that it is not worth the paper on which it is written. This statement applies as much to standard costing as to any other measure of performance. Properly used, standard costing can provide much useful information regarding operating efficiency. However, if incorrect standards are set, or excessive time is spent investigating the reasons for even the slightest variance, to the detriment of the achievement of the overall objectives of the company, then such a system can easily do more harm than good.

96

Chapter 10

Budgeting

A convenient definition of a budget is as follows:

'A budget is an organized statement of expected income and expenditure for a definite future period, usually a month or a year, made in order to assist in controlling expenditures, and to provide a criterion for judging performance during the period' (A.S.M.E.).

The operative word in the above definition is 'expected'. There are many examples of firms which base their budgets on an ideal situation, where all the market forces are assumed to operate to the advantage of the company. Under such circumstances the validity of the final budget must be highly suspect.

To be effective, any information presented to management must conform to the qualities of *impartiality*, *consistency*, *reliability* and *realism*. Walter Chrysler once said that any fool could produce a budget, but it took a very wise man to produce a budget which was realistic.

A budget is a plan, generally expressed in financial terms, of what an organization expects to happen. It is a statement of intent, and every person who will be held accountable for his own particular contribution to its achievement must be involved in its preparation. Further, since it is a statement of intent, the expected results must be capable of achievement. No sensible motor manufacturer would specify that a new model of car will reach 120 m.p.h. without checking that the resources under the bonnet are adequate. Yet many top executives are apparently content to stipulate that their firms will achieve a given saving – say 5 per cent – in numbers employed over a given budget year, without ever checking that this is feasible. When challenged on this point, one chief executive said that it was a waste of time asking his subordinates what savings they could make, as they would never admit to any, for fear of being condemned as currently inefficient. This is the sort of comment which superficially appears to be logical, but which in reality indicates a lack of understanding of human motivation. The vast majority of people who are in responsible jobs are very conscious of the need for efficiency, and their experience gives them a shrewd idea of where cost reductions are possible and where they are not. To be given encouragement to suggest possible savings, and all possible aid to achieve them, makes most people determined to get results. To be told what savings they are to make, frequently without any consultation whatsoever, is hardly an effective method of ensuring success.

Many managers will admit to having received, at one time or another in their career, an edict that they must reduce staff by a given percentage. Such edicts are not uncommon when a company is faced with inadequate profit margins. Saving labour is always a convenient and easily understood way of reducing costs. So, for that matter, is the curtailment of training, cutting down the intake of apprentices, and reducing advertising. All these are easy to do, and easy to cost. They may also be disastrous in the long term, in spite of producing savings in the short.

Because it is so simple to see that the salary bill for a company amounts to, say, £100,000 per annum, it is also simple to calculate that a 10 per cent saving in numbers would represent a cost reduction of £10,000. (The fallacy here is the assumption that the 90 per cent of those who remained would not demand more money, either for more work, or to compensate for lack of security.) So the edict goes forth. Reduce staff numbers by 10 per cent. Now, assuming that a company is reasonably efficient, it is rare for it to be able to reduce staff without giving up certain activities. It is equally rare for top management to be forthcoming regarding which activities are to be discontinued. Consequently, it is likely that every department will be told to reduce numbers by the arbitrary 10 per cent. Unfortunately, this completely overlooks the fact that some departments could well be reduced by 20 per cent, some departments closed down completely, while others ought to be increased by 20 per cent. The trouble is, it is not easy to agree on which departments are over or under staffed, and by default the general saving of 10 per cent has to be implemented, often to the detriment of the ability of the firm to achieve results.

It must not be inferred from the above that a labour-saving exercise is likely to be abortive. Far from it. The point to be made is that the probability of achieving results is much enhanced if those directly concerned are consulted, and are able to advise and agree on what is feasible, and how it is to be achieved. Consultation does not mean asking people what should be done. It does mean explaining the objective, discussing ways and means of reaching it, and agreeing a plan of action.

In the days before their merger with Schweppes, Cadbury Bros., the well-known firm of chocolate manufacturers in Bournville, had no less than twelve managing directors. On being apprised of this fact, students of organization theory used to throw up their hands in horror, muttering about the impossibility of providing firm direction without a unified command. Yet Cadbury's were very successful. They reached Board decisions through a consensus, on the old Quaker principle of general participation. Once a decision had been reached, each managing director did all within his power to ensure that it was translated into successful action.

Without Quaker antecedents, it is unlikely that many firms would be able successfully to adopt the Cadbury system. Nevertheless, it did have certain advantages, not least in the creation of a deep sense of involvement. Involvement – which implies full personal commitment to a project, and being accountable for its attainment – is an indispensable factor in effective budgeting.

If we assume that the usual budget period covers one year, the first stage is to decide on the sales forecast for that year. This forecast should not set out the sales which the company *could* achieve without any tiresome constraints such as labour shortages, plant breakdowns, or quality problems. Rather should it show the sales the company *expects* to achieve, after due consideration has been given to the effect of all likely restricting factors.

In some companies, the sales forecast is the result of an inspired guess, being a statement of the overall value of sales, at current prices, that the directors *think* will be achieved. In others, the forecast is the end result of a detailed and exhaustive statistical examination, product by product and market by market, of the many factors which are likely to affect the business in the budget year. Assumptions – and it must be remembered that every action of management is the result of an assumption – are made regarding market share, and anticipated rates of growth, and consideration given to possible government actions (such as purchase tax), which could affect consumer demand. When these have been evaluated, the wise company will convene a meeting of its sales staff, including the representatives, to discuss the statistical forecast, to modify it where detailed personal knowledge warrants a change, and to agree the expected sales for the year ahead, both on an annual and a monthly basis. Seasonal fluctuations must obviously be considered when discussing monthly results, since many industries have a trade that varies over the year, and due allowance must be made for this. Perhaps the best known example of seasonability is the British fireworks industry, where a high percentage of home sales are concentrated over a few weeks between the middle of October and November 5th, Guy Fawkes Day.

Having agreed the sales forecast, the next steps in budgeting are to decide production methods, to check that sufficient capacity is available to produce goods in accordance with the requirements of the sales forecast, and to estimate the total costs which will be incurred over the year. Finally, assumptions must be made regarding asset movements, including such items as capital expenditure, and changes in stock levels, whether of raw materials, work in progress or finished stocks. With this information, the Accounts Department is able to synthesize a forecast profit and loss account for the budget period.

The precise extent to which budgets are used in industry is not easy to assess, although a recent P.E.P. survey* records that thirty out of forty-seven firms visited by P.E.P. research workers operated a system of budgetary control. Whatever may be the true proportion, it does appear that the majority of firms prepare budgets, although in many cases the resulting figures are little more than a formalized statement of sales, cost of sales, and residual profit.

It is curious how few chief executives are prepared to commit themselves to a statement of the profit they wish their company to make at a given level of sales and capital employed. Asking the question 'What profit do you want?' frequently results in the answer, 'As much as possible.' Such an answer is, of course, singularly unhelpful, since not only would it be a bad commercial policy to operate on this basis, but it would also be difficult to measure performance, since the objective is not quantified.

* *Thrusters and Sleepers*, Allen and Unwin.

It is rarely a good thing for a company to make an excessive profit, even if market conditions permit it to do so. Admittedly, in the short term, a company may appear to be doing well by charging high prices, but there is a danger that, by doing so, it could be jeopardizing its long-term prospects. One reason for this is that a company which has developed a successful product will inevitably find that other companies are eager to enter the market, and to have a share of the profits which are being made. Under normal circumstances, money is nearly always available for investing in a project which offers a good return, and a product which attracts customers will also attract firms wishing to make it. One is reminded of the number of companies who designed hydraulic pit props in the early 1950s, spurred on by the hopes of sharing the large market created by the inspiration and foresight of Sir George Dowty. Among these companies were a safe manufacturer, a marine engineering firm, and a small company owned by a coal merchant!

An original product does not remain original for long, however well protected by patents. A specialized product, relying on the experience of employees and the expertise of technicians, does not remain specialized for long. A customer who buys a product which yields a high profit margin must inevitably question whether he should make the product himself, rather than purchase it as a bought-in component. In this context, Sir Leonard Crossland, when he was Director of Purchasing at Ford of England, once said that he did not object if Ford's suppliers made a 15 per cent profit on their capital employed. If they made 20 per cent they were making too much. If 25 per cent was possible, Ford would make the product themselves.

When assessing profit levels, a company should be clear regarding the profit it wishes to make. At no time is this more appropriate than at the review of the budget estimates.

In every budget, the value of sales is an estimate, as are the costs relating to raw materials, purchases, wages, salaries and other fixed expenses. None of these is known with certainty; all are based on extrapolation of the past and assumption regarding the future. No company can state with certainty that any forecast regarding the future will come true – although judging by the comments of some company chairmen who have been subjected to a takeover bid, it would appear that the gift of prophecy is not dead. There is, however, one figure which every company should be able to specify with great exactness,

101

and that is the level of profit it wishes to make at the budget level of sales. This may be expressed in several ways, such as return on capital, as a percentage of sales, or as a function of the Added Value. This profit, the objective profit, should be clearly defined, so that those who are responsible for the effective operation of the company have the objective clearly in their minds.

There are two schools of thought regarding budgets. The first insists that a budget should be realistic, showing what a company *expects* to happen, the end result being an expected profit. The second insists, equally vehemently, that a budget should be idealistic, showing what a company *wants* to happen, the end result being an objective profit.

A suitable way of resolving the conflict between realism and idealism is to adopt a method of budgeting which incorporates both – the expected (the probable) and the desired (the possible). The procedure is quite simple, and consists of budgeting in two stages. Each stage assumes the same volume of sales, expressed in terms of current selling prices. Firstly, the *probable* budget is prepared, production, selling distribution and general administration costs being estimated by some suitable and realistic procedure. The end result of these various estimates will be a cash flow and a profit. Occasionally it happens that this profit will be acceptable to the Board, in which case the budget would be approved and issued to those concerned. More frequently, the profit is not acceptable, perhaps because the cash flow is inadequate for forward commitments, and the second stage of budgeting is then initiated.

The second stage begins with a skeleton profit and loss account containing two figures, namely forecast sales at the top, and objective profit at the bottom. Starting from the objective profit, the budget officer, in collaboration with the appropriate managers, works through every item of cost set out in the first stage, or probable budget, constructing the cost reduction programme in the process. It may, for example, be agreed that labour productivity can be increased by improved methods. If so, the savings are calculated for incorporation in the cost reduction programme, and the revised labour cost inserted in the budget. This sequence continues through all the items of cost. This done, the revised total cost is added to the objective profit. The sum of these two represents the sales revenue needed to produce the desired profit. If this is greater than the revenue quoted in the first-stage budget, then a price increase is required.

A decision to increase prices can never be lightly taken. If, having exhausted all other possibilities, it is the only way to reach the objective, then it is better to agree an increase as a matter of policy at the time of budgeting, rather than in haste half way through an unsatisfactory year.

The two-stage budget sequence can be expressed diagramatically as follows:

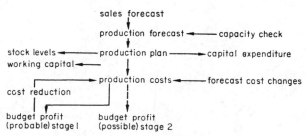

It has been suggested that two-stage budgeting is quite unnecessary, since a company can go straight through to the objective profit, incorporating cost reductions and price increases, and eliminating the first stage altogether. This can undoubtedly be done, and certainly is done by a number of companies. The reason for not doing it is that it tends to produce a statement with a fairly low probability of achievement. This is a bad thing, not only for top management, who may not fully realize the magnitude of the assumptions on which it is based, but also for the line managers, who are likely to realize only too well the pious hopes involved in the cost reductions.

The philosophy behind the two-stage budget is that the first stage represents a statement of intent which is based on realistic assumptions, and which should have a high probability of attainment. The second stage aims to set out the results which must be achieved if the desired profit is to be reached. It must be stressed that this second stage of budgeting will include certain assumptions regarding the selling prices which will apply, and the cost reductions which will be achieved during the budget period. These assumptions may or may not be valid under actual operating conditions.

Budgeting is the art of forecasting the probable. Disillusion can result from optimistic statements which are never matched by results, and company chairmen have been known to express surprise at the massive cost reductions regularly claimed by their companies, which somehow never seem to be translated into improved profits!

A good budget will provide management with a realistic statement against which actual performance can be measured. A bad budget, based on inaccurate or optimistic assumptions, can do more harm than good.

Chapter 11

Budgetary Control

The task of management is to decide what needs to be done, how it is to be done, to initiate action, and to verify results. The system of control may thus be itemized as follows:

1. Decide on the *objective*.
2. *Plan* to meet the objective.
3. Institute *action* to fulfil the plan.
4. *Measure* progress towards the objective.
5. *Compare* actual results with desired results.
6. Initiate *corrective* action where necessary.

Information is the medium of control. The essential characteristic of an effective management control system is that it should provide the right information to the right people at the right time and at the right cost. This may seem axiomatic, but examples could be quoted of information systems which regularly contravene one or more of these principles. Among the complaints frequently made by executives about the information presented to them are that it comes too late for action, that it presents a false picture of events, and that too much of it is concerned with trivialities.

There is always a temptation, particularly in the larger companies, for information to proliferate, and for senior executives to assume that the more information they have regarding the operations of the business, the better their decisions will be. In theory, this sounds eminently sensible. After all, it is no more than the scientific principle of assembling the facts, studying the facts, and deciding on a course of action. Unfortunately for the theorists, business decisions can rarely be taken simply as a result of evaluating facts and figures. The same applies to most of the really important decisions which have been taken through-out history. If, for example, the British Government had reached a decision in 1940 based on a study of the facts of the situation and noth-ing else, there is little doubt that the decision would have been taken to make peace with Nazi Germany. All the facts pointed to the futility of continued resistance. Fortunately for Britain, the decision to fight on was taken in spite of the facts. The decision was mainly based on a refusal to admit defeat, and a supreme confidence in the ability of the British people to win through to ultimate victory.

Facts and figures have an important part to play in the decision-making process. The danger is that people succumb to the temptation to seek out 95 per cent of the facts relating to a given situation, when, more often than not, 80 per cent would be sufficient. Fact-finding is a time-consuming operation, and the time element is all-important in business.

Several years ago, an important American company decided that it should start operations in Britain. It therefore approached a large British group, with a view to promoting a joint United Kingdom-United States company. The large British group was willing, but wished to make sure that the market was available for the proposed product. It therefore commissioned its Market Research department to examine and report on the prospects.

Nine months later, the American company, having heard no more, concluded that the British were disinterested. Consequently, the American Vice President in charge of Marketing flew over to England, and conducted an extensive three-week survey, visiting some 80 per cent of the prospective customers, and all the potential raw material suppliers. As a result of this visit, the Americans decided to go ahead on their own. Out of courtesy they informed their prospective British partner, only to be told that the British company were very interested indeed, and hoped to conclude their market survey during the next three months!

The outcome of this narrative of thorough fact-finding was that, when the British compared notes with the Americans, it was evident that the British had taken nine months to obtain 90 per cent of the facts which they set out to achieve, while the American Vice President had taken three weeks to obtain an estimated 80 per cent. Both parties agreed that the British were virtually no better placed to make a decision to enter the market with their 90 per cent facts than the Americans with their 80 per cent. Both considered that there were good prospects for a joint venture, and that they would succeed if there was the will to succeed. A joint company was therefore formed, and production commenced just at the start of the United Kingdom recession of 1966. Although the company is now profitable, there is every indication that the heavy losses which were incurred in 1966-7 would never have happened if the decision to start operations had been made six months earlier, when market conditions for a new entrant were absolutely right.

Timing is of the utmost importance in effective decision-making. A decision which is right today may be wrong tomorrow. Management must constantly be on the alert to locate new opportunities, and it is the exploitation of such opportunities, at the right time and the right cost, which makes for a successful enterprise. Good timing is rarely based on facts. It is a matter of judgment, of flair, of intuition. Walter Bagehot, the great nineteenth-century economist, frequently made the point that, however inexplicable it might be, there undoubtedly was such a thing as intuition. He was convinced that some men had a flair for taking the right decisions, even in the face of the facts, and it was this flair which differentiated the great from the mediocre. This is, nevertheless, a principle which could be much abused.

Information based on facts is essential for the control of any business. However, care must be taken lest too much information causes a mental blockage. All managers have only a limited time in which to assimilate facts and figures, and if too much is supplied – particularly if the manager remains unconvinced of its validity – there is a real danger that the essentials will be overlooked. Napoleon once said that a constitution should be brief and obscure. He might also have said that a control system should be brief and precise.

Every manager is a receiver of information. To be effective, he must be able to assimilate it, to understand it, and to act on it. This applies to all areas of activity, and particularly to the measurement of performance. One of the major grumbles about budgetary control is that a budget, perhaps prepared many months before, can hardly be valid under altered circumstances.

It will be recalled that a budget is a statement of intent. It is based on a set of carefully related assumptions regarding such parameters as selling prices, material costs, wage rates and so forth. If the value of

107

even one parameter alters, then this tends to set off a chain reaction affecting other parameters, thus causing doubts to be raised regarding the accuracy of the entire budget. One way of dealing with this situation is to revise and reissue the budget. This, of course, is a time-consuming operation, and one which is rarely undertaken. Consequently, over a period of months, many budgets become less and less useful for control purposes, while less and less attention is paid to the operating variances, on the simple argument that, if the budget is inaccurate, then the variances also must be inaccurate.

An effective system of budgetary control can make a powerful contribution to the management of a business. Some companies are content to budget in very general terms, perhaps just showing sales, labour costs and overheads in their budget statement. Others go into considerable detail, analysing and classifying dozens of major and minor expenses, including such items as travelling expenses, bad debts, printing, stationery, royalties and salesmen's commission. The danger of budgeting in too great detail is that, for the purpose of control, it is easy to lose sight of the essentials. The art of successful management is to be able to locate the essentials, make decisions, and achieve results through other people. The location of essentials is always made easier if information systems are designed to concentrate on a few really important operating features of a business, and this applies particularly to budgetary control.

A simple form of budgetary control is shown in Table 21, which is a hypothetical example but not untypical of companies with relatively undeveloped costing systems.

TABLE 21: ARGEE ENGINEERING – OCTOBER, 1970

	Actual £	*Budget* £	*Variance* £
Sales	19,800	22,000	2,200 under
Materials	9,500	10,400	900 under
	10,300	11,600	
Labour	3,050	3,380	330 under
	7,250	8,220	
Overheads	5,700	5,600	100 over
Profit	1,550	2,620	1,070 under

The presentation shown in Table 21 is not very helpful for the purpose of control, since the variances are almost meaningless because actual sales differ from the budget. Obviously, if actual sales are less than the budget, actual expenses should also be less than the budget. What the management of Argee Engineering would obviously wish to know is what the actual expenses should have been for the level of sales achieved.

A commonly used method of compensating for a level of sales which is different from that budgeted is to adopt what is known as 'flexing'. To flex a budget means that the variable items of cost are adjusted in proportion to the ratio Actual Sales : Budget Sales. To illustrate this point let us suppose budget sales are £20,000 per month, for budget raw material costs of £10,000. If in a given month sales are only £18,000 – or 90 per cent of budget – the flexed raw material costs should be 90 per cent of budget also – that is £9,000.

Table 21 is of very limited use as it stands. By flexing, it becomes a much more significant document, as is shown in Table 22.

TABLE 22: ARGEE ENGINEERING – OCTOBER, 1970 – FLEXED BUDGET

Expense Classification		Actual	Budget (unflexed)	Budget (flexed)	Variance against flexed budget
		£	£	£	£
	Sales	19,800	22,000	19,800	
Variable	Materials	9,500	10,400	9,400	100 over
		10,300	11,600	10,400	
Variable	Prod. Labour	3,050	3,380	3,050	Nil
		7,250	8,220	7,350	
Variable	Overheads – Variable	2,000	1,900	1,710	290 over
Fixed	– Fixed	3,700	3,700	3,700	Nil
	Profit	1,550	2,620	1,940	−390

Table 22 shows the costs which should have applied at the actual level of activity. Furthermore, it shows that the profit is £390 less than it should have been, after allowing for the reduced activity compared with the budget. The balance of the difference between actual and budget profit, namely £680, is attributed to the lower level of sales.

A flexed budget is helpful for control purposes, and such a budget can be used as a primary measure of performance.

A method of budgetary control which enables information to be presented in a concise but understandable form is based on the use of expense ratios. Having decided, at the budgeting stage, the value of sales and the raw material and conversion costs, a series of ratios are developed. These ratios represent the percentage to sales of materials, purchases and labour. Obviously, only the variable costs can be budgeted in terms of percentage to sales. The percentage of fixed costs to sales will vary depending on the actual sales achieved. The assumption here is that variable costs do vary in proportion to output, while fixed costs remain unchanged whatever the output. Table 23 illustrates this procedure. Note that the budgeted Added Value is clearly indicated, to provide a measure of the anticipated company net income and output.

TABLE 23: XYZ LTD. BUDGET COST RATIOS – PERIOD IV, 1970

	Budget		Budget Cost Ratios
	£	£	
Sales value	100,000	100·0	
Raw materials	55,000	55·0	55·0%
	45,000	45·0	
Purchases	9,000	9·0	9·0%
Added Value	36,000	36·0	
Production labour	12,000	12·0	12·0%
Contribution	24,000	24·0	
Fixed expenses	14,000	14·0	
Profit	10,000	10·0	
	Added Value: Sales		36·0%
	Labour: Added Value		33·3%

Two key ratios are included in Table 23. These are Added Value : Sales and Labour : Added Value. As a general rule, a product which has a great deal of work applied in converting it from raw material to finished form will show a high Added Value : Sales Ratio. A product where little work is applied will show a low Added Value : Sales Ratio.

The ratio Labour : Added Value has great significance in the appraisal of company performance, as has' already been discussed in Chapter 8. An increase in this ratio over time is always indicative of a rise in wage costs per unit of output, and as such demands a comprehensive investigation to ascertain the precise causes.

Referring again to Table 23; once the significant ratios have been established, they are subsequently used for calculating the budget level of expenses against the actual sales achieved throughout the budget year. In companies operating this procedure it is customary for a monthly profit and loss account to be prepared. The actual sales and operating costs are tabulated, and the budget costs calculated in £ sterling by multiplying the actual sales value by the relevant budget cost ratio.

The method of calculating budget expenses through the application of budget cost ratios is shown in Table 24.

TABLE 24: XYZ LTD. TRADING STATEMENT – PERIOD IV, 1970

	Actual £	Budget £	Budget Cost Ratio %	Budgeted Expenses £	Variance Over/Under £
Sales Value	120,000	100,000			
Raw Materials	68,000		55·0	66,000	2,000 over
	52,000				
Purchases	10,600		9·0	10,800	200 under
Added Value	41,400				
Production Labour	15,200		12·0	14,400	800 over
Contribution	26,200				
Fixed Expenses	14,200			14,000	200 over
Profit	12,000	10,000			2,800 loss

Increase in profit due to increased volume		4,800 gain
Net profit variance		2,000 gain

	Actual	Budget
Added Value: Sales	34·5%	36·0%
Labour: Added Value	36·7%	33·3%

111

It will be noted that increased sales brought a profit gain of £4,800 against budget. However, the increased operating expenses on this activity showed an adverse variance of £2,800, thus resulting in a net profit increase of £2,000 for the period.

Budgetary control based on expense ratios have many applications, and are both easily understood and easy to apply. An interesting extension of this technique is to develop ratios which show how the company income (the Added Value) must be allocated in order to achieve the budget profit. These ratios are prepared at the budgetary stage, and represent how the company income is being spent. By comparing the actual ratios with the budget ratios, the areas of profit shortfall are clearly indicated.

The firm of Wrogerson & Co.* uses control ratios based on Added Value for the appraisal of company performance. Wrogerson's is a private company, with five full-time executive directors. The Board meets on the third Monday of each month, and a regular item on the agenda is the discussion of the trading results. The company prepares its budgets in October for the twelve-month period commencing on January 1st of the following year. The budgets are prepared in two stages, by the procedure described in Chapter 11. Firstly, the sales for the year are agreed, and the related costs calculated. This gives the expected profit. Secondly, the profit which the company *wants* to make is set out, together with the costs and selling prices necessary for the achievement of this profit. In both cases a series of Sales and Added Value ratios are prepared, which form the bases for the monthly appraisal of results.

Wrogerson's objective is to make 15 per cent pre-tax profit on capital employed, when the factory is reasonably well loaded. The definition of 'reasonably well loaded' is somewhat arbitrary, but is usually equivalent to operating at about 85 per cent of full capacity.

The monthly trading statement is presented in £ sterling and in percentages. The actual results are compared with the budget (expected) and the budget (objective).

Table 25 is an abbreviated form of the presentation of results expressed in percentages.

* See Chapter 8, p. 83.

TABLE 25: WROGERSON & CO., TRADING STATEMENT RATIOS,
PERIODS I AND II, 1970

I. *Sales Margins*

| | Budget | | Actual | | | | | |
	Expected %	Objective %	Jan. %	Feb. %	March %	April %	May %	June %
Sales	100·0	100·0	100·0	100·0	100·0	100·0	100·0	100·0
Materials	57·2	56·8	58·1	58·2	58·1	58·0	57·2	57·8
	42·8	43·2	41·9	41·8	41·9	42·0	42·8	42·2
Purchases	10·4	10·1	9·6	10·1	10·2	10·3	10·4	10·3
Added Value	32·4	33·1	32·3	31·7	31·7	31·7	32·4	31·9
Prod. Labour	10·7	10·4	11·0	10·8	10·8	10·7	10·9	11·0
Contribution	21·7	22·7	21·3	20·9	20·9	21·0	21·5	20·9
Fixed	14·0	13·5	13·2	14·6	14·0	14·3	14·7	13·9
Profit	7·7	9·2	8·1	6·3	6·9	6·7	6·8	7·0
A.V.: *Sales*	32·4	33·1	32·3	31·7	31·7	31·7	32·4	31·9
Lab.: A.V.	33·0	31·4	34·0	34·0	34·0	33·8	33·7	34·5

II. *Added Value Margins*

| | Budget | | Actual | | | | | |
	Expected %	Objective %	Jan. %	Feb. %	March %	April %	May %	June %
Added Value	100·0	100·0	100·0	100·0	100·0	100·0	100·0	100·0
Prod. Labour	33·0	31·4	34·0	34·0	34·0	33·8	33·7	34·5
Maintenance Labour	3·7	3·6	3·6	3·8	3·8	3·8	3·6	3·6
Staff Salaries	16·2	16·1	16·2	17·3	17·1	16·7	15·9	15·6
Wages and Salaries	52·9	51·1	53·8	55·1	54·9	54·3	53·2	53·7
All other Fixed	23·3	21·3	21·2	25·0	23·4	24·5	25·8	24·3
Profit	23·8	27·6	25·0	19·9	21·7	21·2	21·0	22·0

III. *Break-even, etc.*								
Break-even Ratio	64½%	60½%	62½%	69%	67%	68%	68%	67%
Capacity Utilization	89%	90%	88%	83%	82%	85%	87%	89%
Labour Productivity	£2,100	£2,240	£1,980	£1,900	£1,920	£1,990	£2,000	£2,010

N.B. Break-even Ratio $= \dfrac{\text{Break-even Sales}}{\text{Actual Sales}} \times 100$

Capacity Utilization $= \dfrac{\text{Actual Sales}}{\text{Capacity Sales}} \times 100$

Labour Productivity = Added Value per Employee—£ p.a.

113

The ratios in Table 25 reveal, simply and quickly, areas of developing weakness. For example, it is particularly evident that the production labour costs per unit of output are not at all satisfactory. In June, for example, the actual Labour: Added Value ratio was 34·5%, instead of the budget (expected) ratio of 33·0%. Assuming no change in hourly rates of pay, the labour productivity in June would have had to be increased by some $4\frac{1}{2}$% in order to achieve the expected ratio of 33·0%.

A well-designed budgetary control system will help management to ask the right questions. It will not, and cannot of itself, provide the right answers. The latter are the result of managerial flair, sound human judgment and effective decisions.

Chapter 12

Pricing for Profit

Prices, and their effect on profits, are a matter of concern not only to capitalist but also to communist societies. Professor Piotr Alampiev, writing in 1970 in the Moscow magazine *New Times*, commented that the Soviet Union was of the opinion that the prices it was obtaining for crude oil, gas, raw materials and agricultural produce in Comecon were not high enough, and that the exporters of machinery were making great profits. In the article, he conceded that he was expressing the views of the Soviet Union. The exporters of machinery thought just the opposite.

Daniel Nimer, a leading U.S. marketing economist, has argued persuasively that British industry consistently underestimates the image and quality of its products in overseas markets, and as a result undercharges for its goods. In this context, the role of pricing in the marketing mix is to create and maximize profits. Because British companies do not price properly, their profits are too low, and new product development is restricted. Marketing men must break with tradition, and not passively accept prices based on a percentage mark-up on total cost.

Irrespective of the social system of a country, logical pricing policies are an indispensable condition of profitable operation. This may cause surprise to people who are well aware of the need for profits in a capitalist society, but who somehow feel that they are unnecessary for communist societies. This misconception may arise from the fact that communist societies are not particularly good at making profits – hence the increased concentration on economic reforms to stimulate the profit motive which were a feature of Soviet industrial life in the late 1960s.

About one hundred years ago, Karl Marx, who was not altogether unsympathetic to the idea of a communist society, wrote a thesis called

115

Critique of the Gotha Programme. In this he argued that the price of a given product should first have deducted from it the cost of the materials used in its manufacture. Next, one should deduct a part of the price as a contribution towards the salaries of the non-productive personnel in society – scientists, teachers, doctors, nurses, administrators and so forth. Then one should set aside a sum for the provision of capital for new enterprises. Only then should the remainder be divided among the working men in proportion to the expenditure of their labour and their skills.

Marx was very insistent that the national income was made up of 'essential product' and 'surplus product'. The difference between a communist and a capitalist society was not that the former should avoid making surplus product, but rather that, under communism, this surplus product should be distributed to society at large and not to capitalists in particular.

To underline the statement that profit is essential to all societies, it is perhaps worth recalling that the XIIth Party Congress of the Soviet Union, held in 1923, passed a resolution stating that the question of creating profit in industry was the question of the fate of Soviet economic power, for an industry working unprofitably could not become the foundation of a new economic system.

Profits result from transactions. To be fully acceptable, a transaction must satisfy both parties. The vendor must be satisfied that the price is acceptable, giving him an appropriate return for the work he has done and the risks he has taken. The purchaser must be satisfied that he is obtaining value for his money. In this context, value is a subjective measurement of the factors which make a product desirable in the market. A sale is made on the basis of price, service and quality. The price a prospective purchaser is prepared to pay for a product depends on his assessment of the service and quality he will obtain. Service relates to reliable delivery performance, ease of maintenance, availability of spares, facilities for repair, and so forth. Quality relates not only to fitness for purpose, but also to style, appearance, craftsmanship, and that indefinable characteristic known as image.

In a competitive economy, free from interference at government level, the pricing mechanism has two main functions. Firstly, it provides a means of rationing goods and services which are in short supply by raising the price and hence reducing demand. Secondly, it enables the vast number of people comprising the market to make their wishes

116

known, thus directing the resources of the nation towards those products, or services, which are most wanted.

At the level of company affairs, an effective pricing policy should provide a means of evaluating how highly a customer rates a given product. If it is rated at a level which provides the manufacturer with an acceptable income following a sale, then both parties to the transactions will be satisfied. If the income is not acceptable, then the manufacturer will be dissatisfied. Implicit in this is the assumption that the vendor is aware of the price he wants for his product and, perhaps equally important, the minimum price he is prepared to accept. In the case of a company producing a large number of disparate products such awareness is not easy to achieve.

Whether communist or capitalist, an enterprise must make a profit if it is to survive. No price can be considered acceptable if it does not result in a profit. At this stage it is perhaps worth mentioning that we must not confuse profit with profit margin. Profit is a relationship between total income and total expenditure, and is conventionally expressed in cash terms. Profit margin is a ratio. In almost every instance when a businessman talks of profitability he means profit margin, expressed as the percentage of profit to sales turnover. Thus a 10 per cent profit margin would imply that a given transaction has resulted in a profit which is equal to 10 per cent of the value of sales. If a motor vehicle costs £900 to make, and is sold for £1,000, the profit would be £100 and the profit margin 10 per cent.

It can be misleading to speak of the profitability of a given product in terms of the profit margin, since by itself this ratio does not necessarily indicate the profit resulting over time from the sales of that product. For example, article 'A' might have a profit margin of 10 per cent, and article 'B' a margin of 5 per cent. At first sight we might assume that 'A' is twice as profitable as 'B', but before accepting this, we must find out more about the relative sales of 'A' and 'B'. Our investigation might show that 'B' has an annual sales value five times that of 'A'. This would then alter the assessment of profitability, as shown in the following calculation.

	Profit Margin (Profit: Sales – %)	Annual Sales £	Annual Profit £
Article 'A'	10	10,000	1,000
Article 'B'	5	50,000	2,500

On this basis, 'B' is two and a half times as profitable as 'A'.

Irrespective of the way in which a company's profitability is expressed, the profit potential depends on its ability to price its products so that they provide value not only to the customer (who would not purchase them if they didn't) but also to the company itself. In other words, *good pricing results in good profits.*

One method of pricing which is often used is based on the addition of a fixed percentage to total cost. An article costing 100 units would thus be priced by adding a predetermined amount – say 15 per cent – to the cost, thus arriving at a price of 115 units. This procedure can be quite effective, although it has serious disadvantages when a company is manufacturing a wide range of products, or when it uses raw materials of varying cost, as, for example, steel and copper. Under such conditions a fixed mark-up on total cost is not a good principle.

Suppose a firm makes steel lamp standards and copper lamp standards. The conversion cost in each case might be the same, say 50 units, but the raw material cost would be quite different, possibly 50 units for the steel, and 500 units for the copper. A 15 per cent mark-up on cost would give selling prices as follows:

	Steel	*Copper*
Raw Material	50	500
Conversion	50	50
Total Cost	100	550
Mark-up @ 15%	15	82½
Selling Price	115	632½

In the case of the steel lamp standard, the profit is 15 units for a conversion cost of 50 units (or 30 per cent). In the case of the copper, the profit is 82½ units, also for a conversion cost of 50 (or 165 per cent). It is most unlikely that the competitors of the firm making copper lamp standards would allow it to make profits of this magnitude!

To be able to price effectively by adding a percentage to total cost presupposes that this cost is known. Herein lies a serious difficulty. The total cost of an article can only be estimated in relation to the production of a specified number of articles. It is easy to say what the costs *were* for a given product, knowing the number which have been produced. It is not at all easy to say what the costs *will* be, not knowing the numbers to be produced. Yet, since prices are generally required for the future and not for the past, a decision has to be made regarding anticipated numbers, for without such a decision no total cost can be prepared.

As with every other company policy, a pricing policy cannot be devised without a clear definition of objectives. These must be spelled out, possibly in terms of return on capital, cash flow, profit per share, or some other suitable figure. It is not good enough to proclaim, as did one company chairman in his annual report to shareholders, that '. . . the Group must have as its objective a turnover by 1974 of not less than £100 million.' One is tempted to ask whether the Chairman would consider the objective achieved if operating expenses also reached £100 million by 1974!

The primary requirement of a successful pricing policy is that it should result in a given level of profitability. Many other factors must be considered and incorporated in the policy, among these being:

Delegation
1. Decide who has discretionary authority for setting prices, and within what limits.
2. Decide who prescribes price levels outside these limits.

Pricing
1. Decide the pricing framework. Should there be discounts based on quantity? On loyalty? On preferred sizes? On standard specifications?
2. Decide whether export prices will be similar to or different from home prices.
3. Institute a system for dealing with price queries and price changes.

Control
1. Maintain records of
    (*a*) Enquiries received.
    (*b*) Orders received.
    (*c*) Prices quoted.
    (*d*) Competition prices.
2. Set up systems for measuring the effectiveness of salesmen in achieving the prices the company wants for its products.

Statistics
1. Record market information, and all relevant statistics published by the Board of Trade, Trade Associations, Trade Journals and the national press.

The above list is not comprehensive, but it does itemize typical factors

119

which must be given due thought and attention. The degree of statistical sophistication will obviously vary from company to company, but even the smallest companies are likely to find that the information published in the monthly *Digest of Statistics** can be of assistance.

A business must satisfy human needs, otherwise no one will buy its products. It must also maintain a sufficient surplus of total income over total expenditure, so as to ensure survival, replacement of capital equipment, and the exploitation of opportunities. The primary responsibility of every chief executive is to seek out new opportunities, to make the best use of the resources available to him, and to satisfy himself that total income is acceptable for the requirements of the company.

In certain businesses, where the value of the product is high – such as shipbuilding, rolling mill construction, or motor vehicles – the chief executive may be able to vet and agree every selling price. Presumably he will have a formalized pricing policy, and because he is always involved, he will be able to apply this consistently. This is important, particularly since the chief executive is ultimately accountable to the Board of Directors, and, through them, to the shareholders. Harry S. Truman, whom history is revealing as one of the greatest American Presidents of all time, was reputed to have had a notice on his desk which said, 'The buck stops here.' The same applies to chief executives in industry.

If the chief executive is able to discuss and agree every selling price, then he need do no more than be clear in his own mind what he is trying to achieve. In most cases, however, the chief executive is not able to agree every selling price, since businesses are constantly receiving enquiries, preparing estimates, and issuing quotations. If a firm sells its products against a price list, then few pricing decisions are necessary other than to agree the validity of the list. If the company is quoting for business, negotiating with customers, dealing with agents, and trying to export, then no one man can possibly cope with everything. Under such circumstances, the chief executive must ensure that his subordinates are clearly aware of his policy, and that the procedures to be adopted are properly defined and consistently applied.

A large proportion of the goods produced by industry are sold as a result of the enquiry-bid system. A prospective customer who wishes to buy a certain product will send out enquiries to several manufacturers. The latter will then make a bid, that is, will quote for the supply of the

* H.M.S.O.

product; the bid will almost certainly include details of the offered price and delivery, and it may go into considerable detail regarding material specification, design and performance. Having received the bids, the prospective customer evaluates them against the measures of price, service and quality, and makes a decision as to the source of supply.

Let us suppose that ten manufacturers submit bids for a given quantity of an identical product. Even if their production costs are exactly the same, ten different prices could well be quoted. Prices do not necessarily reflect costs. Each company might use a different procedure for converting cost to selling price. Alternatively, some companies might be desperately short of work, and be prepared to reduce profit margins to obtain the business. Again, that most dangerous reason for cutting prices, namely 'prestige', might cause some companies to quote low.

Whatever the reason, it is probable that the ten prices would all be different. The price level of the product as offered in the market would be the mean of the prices quoted, and effectively each bidding company would be trying to quote slightly below this level if they wished to obtain the business. Since the only company knowing this level is the one receiving the bids, obviously the judgment of the bidders regarding market levels is of great importance.

A company can generally increase its market share by quoting appreciably below market price. This strategy requires careful monitoring, since it must be realized that, each time such action is taken, the overall market level is reduced. Thus prices tend to erode, and many good businesses have become very unprofitable due to their frantic efforts to increase sales volume by reducing prices.

On the face of it, one can easily be deluded into thinking that there is a good case for a company accepting business at anything above marginal cost, provided that it has spare productive capacity. 'As long as an order makes some contribution to fixed expenses,' so the argument goes, 'the company is better off taking it than not taking it.' This statement sounds convincing. So it is if nothing else is altered as a result of such action. Unfortunately for the proponents of the argument, it is exceedingly rare for nothing else to be altered. Almost certainly, implementation of such a policy will cause a slow but certain reduction in overall price levels. Furthermore, even the best managed companies tend to forget which jobs in their overall product mix were accepted at low prices. All that they can see in their profit and loss statement is

121

that overall profitability is not acceptable. From this, they erroneously assume that all prices are unsatisfactory, quite overlooking the real fact that it is a minority of jobs, taken at near marginal prices, which are adversely affecting the total result.

A small percentage change in overall prices can result in a large change in profitability. This is illustrated in the following example, where the profitability of Wrogerson & Co.* is examined at different selling price levels.

TABLE 26: WROGERSON & CO., PROFITS/PRICE RELATIONSHIPS, 1970

Budget Fixed Expense ... £24,700
Contribution Rate ... 23·1%

Monthly Profit – £ stg.

Monthly Sales – £	At Budget Prices	At Budget Prices Plus 3%	At Budget Prices Less 3%
150,000	10,000	14,400	5,400
160,000	12,200	17,000	7,500
170,000	14,600	19,700	9,500
(Budget) 180,000	16,500	22,300	11,500
190,000	19,100	24,800	13,500
200,000	21,400	27,400	15,500
Break-even sales	107,000	95,000	123,000

This example shows the disastrous consequences to Wrogerson if, on average, the company allows selling prices to drift downwards by 3 per cent. Instead of the budget profit of £16,500, a profit of only £11,500 will result. On the other hand, if Wrogerson can obtain a 3 per cent increase in prices, other costs being unchanged, then the profit will be £22,300 for sales of £180,000. This relationship between profit and price is further illustrated in Fig. 14. This shows the monthly profit which will accrue to Wrogerson, assuming different levels of price, and budget sales of £180,000 per month. The effect of a 15 per cent increase or decrease in sales value is also shown.

Figure 14 indicates that, if prices have to be reduced by an average of 3 per cent, an *increase* in sales of 15 per cent will be necessary if budget profits are to be maintained. However, if prices can be increased by 4 per cent, similar profits can be earned on a 15 per cent *decrease* in

* See Chapter 9, Table 17.

122

FIGURE 14: PROFIT PRICE RELATIONSHIPS

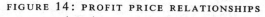

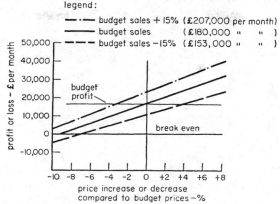

sales. In this respect, Wrogerson is typical of many companies in the engineering sector of industry.

Let us now examine the ways in which Wrogerson might price their products in order to achieve their budget profit of £16,500 per month. Firstly, we will examine the margins, as set out in the Wrogerson objective budget quoted in Table 17.

Wrogerson's objective is to make a profit of £16,500 on total sales of £180,000. The procedure for calculating selling prices must be designed to achieve this, and herein lies the crux of the matter. What procedure should Wrogerson adopt?

It has already been mentioned that a common method of pricing is to add a percentage to total cost. The underlying principle is quite simple. Referring to Table 27, it will be noted that Wrogerson's total costs are £163,500. The objective revenue is £180,000. Thus a mark-up of £16,500 on total cost, or 10·1 per cent, would produce the requisite revenue. Equally, marking up by this percentage every individual cost relating to the hundreds of products made would also produce the desired revenue – assuming always that the products could be sold at these prices.

A second method of pricing is based on the argument that a company must generate sufficient income to produce a gross margin – or contribution to fixed expenses – which is more than sufficient to pay for the fixed expenses. Any surplus represents profit. To produce this contribution, the company must utilize people, providing them with tools, electric power, and other items associated with the variable costs of

123

TABLE 27: WROGERSON & CO., OBJECTIVE MARGINS 1970

(*Variable or Fixed*)		£ stg	%
	Sales	180,000	100·0
V	Raw Materials	102,000	56·5
		78,000	43·5
V	Purchases	18,200	10·1
	Added Value	59,800	33·4
V	Production Labour	18,600	10·3
	Contribution	41,200	23·1
F	Fixed Expenses	24,700	13·7
	Profit	16,500	9·4

Total Costs – Variable = £138,800
    – Fixed   = £ 24,700

Total   £163,500

Added Value: Sales   = 33·4%
Labour: Added Value = 31·0%

production. The contribution is the result of the effective application of these variable items on raw materials. Therefore, according to the protagonists of this method of pricing, raw material and variable production costs should be marked up to give the desired contribution, and hence to derive a selling price. The arithmetic is as follows, using Table 27 costs:

Raw Material Cost	£102,000
Variable expenses (ex. material)	£36,800

	£
Objective contribution	41,200
Raw material mark-up @ 10% (say)	10,200
Balance mark-up	31,000

$$\therefore \text{Variable expense mark-up} = \frac{31,000}{36,000} = 84\%$$

The theory here is that part of the contribution results from marking up raw material by 10 per cent, and the remainder by marking up variable expenses by 84 per cent.

124

It will be appreciated that, once the principles of pricing are understood, numerous ways of marking up costs can be evolved to produce a given result. One further method is worth mentioning, known as unit wage cost pricing. The assumption underlying this system is that a company is in business to create Added Value. The more it creates per employee the higher will be its productivity, and the greater its competitive ability. In most industrialized nations, labour is the scarce resource. Consequently, it is desirable to try and maximize the output achieved from this particular resource, and to plan for a certain minimum return, in terms of Added Value, for every £1 spent on wages. (This is, of course, the same as saying that the ratio Labour : Added Value should not exceed a given figure.)

Unit wage cost pricing derives a selling price by marking up the labour cost by a percentage which will give the desired Added Value. In any cost estimate, the two elements which should be known accurately are Production Labour and Raw Material costs. Any proper costing system will be able to extract these. The remaining variable expenses should also be known reasonably accurately. The fixed expenses will be a guess, depending on the anticipated quantity to be produced. By marking up Production Labour to give a desired Added Value, one is marking up one of the two most reliable costs, the other being raw materials.

Referring again to Table 27, it will be noted that the profit of £16,500 results from an Added Value of £59,800. The Production Labour cost is £18,600. Thus to achieve the Added Value, Production Labour must be marked up by 59,800/18,600, or 320 per cent. This, in brief, is the unit wage cost method of pricing – marking up Production Labour to create the desired Added Value.

It has earlier been stated that different methods of pricing will produce different selling prices. To illustrate this, we will now calculate the selling price of a product, using three different methods. The actual product costs on which the prices will be based are as follows:

	Pence per Piece
Raw materials	51·0
Production Labour	18·2
Variable overheads	18·7
Fixed overheads	25·5
Total Cost	113·4

Using the three pricing procedures and mark-ups previously described in this chapter we have:

Method 1   Cost-Plus Pricing

$$\text{Selling price} = \text{Total Cost} + 10.1\%$$
$$= 113.4 + 10.1\% \text{ of } 113.4$$
$$= 113.4 + 11.5$$
$$= 124.9 \text{ pence per piece} \tag{1}$$

Method 2   Variable Mark-up Pricing

$$\text{Objective Contribution} = 10\% \text{ of raw material cost plus}$$
$$84\% \text{ of variable conversion cost}$$
$$= 10\% \text{ of } 51.0 \text{ plus } 84\% \text{ of } 36.9$$
$$= 36.1 \text{ pence.}$$
$$\text{Selling price} = \text{Contribution} + (\text{Labour} + \text{variables} + \text{material})$$
$$= 36.1 + (18.2 + 18.7 + 51.0)$$
$$= 124.0 \text{ pence per piece.} \tag{2}$$

Method 3   Unit Wage Cost Pricing

$$\text{Objective Added Value} = 320\% \text{ of Production labour}$$
$$= 320\% \text{ of } 18.2$$
$$= 58.1 \text{ pence}$$
$$\text{Selling price} = \text{Added Value} + (\text{Variables} + \text{material})$$
$$= 58.1 + (18.7 + 51.0)$$
$$= 127.8 \text{ pence per piece.} \tag{3}$$

It is evident that each of the above methods has resulted in a different selling price, even though identical costs have been used. It would be quite wrong to suggest that one of these is the best, since we cannot make specific pricing recommendations without a comprehensive knowledge of product range, market conditions, capital investment required and other relevant factors relating to a given firm. Each has its own applications and limitations, but great care must be taken when using a pricing method which does not explicitly include recovery of total cost, such as methods (2) and (3). Both these have proved effective in practice, but they should never be adopted without the advice of an experienced cost accountant. A firm which manufactures products requiring similar man-hours, but processed on machines of vastly different cost, could easily run into trouble if the basis of pricing did not make allowance for this.

A positive pricing policy is an essential feature of managing for profit. Such a policy should define not only the price a company wants for its products, but also the minimum it is prepared to accept. This concept of two prices – objective and minimum – should always be in the minds of the chief executive and members of the sales department. There is no virtue in selling at the wrong price. Anybody can fill a factory to capacity if he consistently undercuts the opposition. The real art of profitable operation lies in defining what a business wants from its commercial transactions, and making sure that it does not accept orders which fail to provide a satisfactory return. As the chairman of Britain's largest engineering group, G.K.N., said at the Annual General Meeting in May 1970, 'To have a wonderful relationship with a customer and put down a bottle of Scotch with him is no good at all unless you have a $12\frac{1}{2}$ per cent mark-up.'

Chapter 13

Incentives for Profit

For as long as man has worked for man, whether the relationship has been one of slavery, serfdom, or master and servant, those organizing work have grappled with the problem of how to obtain more effort from those performing work. At the same time, the latter have tended to avoid giving of their best, in the apparent conviction that there is more to life than consistent and unremitting toil.

Early ideas of employee remuneration were based on the principle of penalty and reward, the underlying assumption being that people at work maximize their own interests, and act accordingly. Thus, if one wants a person to behave in a specific manner, one should make it pleasant for him if he does so, and unpleasant if he does not. This doctrine dominated the strategy of both management and trade unions up to the outbreak of the second world war. As a result, the industrial relationships that developed between employer and employee were based on the concept of a personal bargain, whereby a certain wage was agreed in return for certain work. The self-interest of the individual was assumed to be capable of expression during the bargaining process, but having made a bargain he was expected to abide by it. If he did not, various sanctions were invoked, such as loss of earnings, suspension, or dismissal.

Throughout this stage, there was general acceptance that the relationship was a personal one, in spite of the growth of collective bargaining. Under this system people transferred their individual rights to trade unions, in return for collective power and solidarity.

Later ideas which evolved regarding industrial behaviour assumed that social needs were equally as important as economic needs, and that the need for self-fulfilment, and acceptance by others, was a powerful motivation. This social theory stressed that people at work tend to organize themselves into groups, and to develop a pattern of relationships with their superiors and their colleagues. From these relationships a standard of group behaviour evolves, and it is this standard which is adopted by the individuals, and to which they conform. For example, if a group accepts the unwritten rule that it is undesirable, for fear of rate-cutting, to earn more than, say, £15 per week on the bonus scheme, it is rare for an individual to exceed this amount, however much he may want the extra money.

Proponents of the social theory argued that, with increasing standards of education, people must be enabled to utilize their capacities to the full. In addition to being told what to do, they must also be told why they are to do it, and how their task correlates with the overall objectives of the business.

Theories on human behaviour are extremely interesting, and they are well worth studying in the hope that they may be of assistance in providing at least part of the answer to the question of why people behave as they do. The one thing that can be said with certainty is that people are unpredictable. There is no one right way to deal with them, nor is there one right way to run a factory. The right way can only be decided with the advantage of hindsight. If it produced the desired results it was right.

Management is the art of getting other people to do the things one wants them to do. Management involves motivating people, and it would no doubt be much easier for management control if there were a civilian equivalent of Queen's Regulations available to and enforceable by industry. It might be easier; it certainly would be less effective. Wilfred Brown once said, 'The only real authority we have is that given to us by our subordinates.' Without such authority, no manager can hope to survive in a free society.

Any discussion of human motivation inevitably leads to the question of incentives. To most people, an incentive implies monetary reward, but this is not necessarily so. Incentives may be financial or non-financial.

Incentives are used for three main purposes:

1. To persuade people to come to work.
2. To encourage people to work harder when they are at work.
3. To help people to identify themselves with the objectives of the organization, and hence to work more effectively.

129

1. PERSUADING PEOPLE TO COME TO WORK

Various incentives are commonly used for this purpose, such as the promise of good working conditions, sports facilities, welfare services and guaranteed overtime. In the case of overtime, cause and effect have become completely reversed over the years. Originally, premiums for overtime working were demanded by the trade unions to discourage employers from working their labour force excessive hours. Now, the offer of guaranteed overtime is a bait used by employers to attract labour.

There are critics who consider that British industry could well dispense with overtime altogether. They point out that, irrespective of the length of the basic working week – 40 hours in 1970 – the actual hours worked tend to remain remarkably constant at about 47 per week. They further suggest that, if industry would only pay a reasonable basic wage, so that 47 hours' pay could be earned in 40 hours, people would correspondingly raise their productivity, cut out overtime, and all would benefit.

There is much truth in the argument that people restrict output so as to create overtime. In spite of progressive taxation, the vast majority are pleased to work for premium rates of pay. The big question is whether they would still wish to do so if they were able to earn 47 hours' pay in 40 hours. It seems very probable that they would, particularly where Saturday mornings are concerned. In Britain, social patterns are such that Saturday morning offers no real opportunity for leisure activities. If the man of the house stays at home, he might be involved in housework or shopping, neither of which compares favourably with earning 'time and a half' in a factory. Saturday afternoon, as every personnel manager is well aware, is quite another matter, with television competing with football matches for the favours of the fans.

2. ENCOURAGING PEOPLE TO WORK HARDER

Financial incentives are used almost universally in the constant drive to improve the productivity of labour. Such incentives may be broadly classified under six main headings:

1. Payment by results.
2. Measured daywork.

3. High day rate.
4. Merit rating.
5. Specialized company schemes.
6. Productivity-related schemes.

Each of these is a subject on its own, and each has its devotees. Much has been written on the advantages and disadvantages of the various wage payment systems which have been designed to produce more effort by rewarding hard work, and it is not proposed to discuss these in detail. Suffice it to say that payment by results schemes, relating to the group or individual, are the most frequently encountered incentive payment methods in British industry. A sensibly constructed and equitable payment by results system, whereby the individual is remunerated in proportion to the output he achieves, is one of the best incentives yet evolved. It must, however, be based on proper work measurement, be capable of yielding a fair return, and be readily understood. Further, the employee must be able directly to affect his level of earnings through his own efforts.

Management must never assume that an incentive scheme eliminates the need for supervision. The truth is that any bonus payment system is demanding on those who administer it. The enthusiastic manager will obtain results even from a system which apparently contravenes all the rules. The lazy manager, who relies on the incentive, by itself, to produce results, will fail with the most perfect system yet devised. As Lord Fleck once said, when he was Chairman of I.C.I., 'The heart and core of good industrial management is, as it always has been, the ability to get people to work for you. Wages, hours of work, conditions, amenities, all play a part, but in the last analysis it gets down to character, the personality and example of the people who lead the enterprise.'

3. HELPING PEOPLE TO IDENTIFY THEMSELVES WITH THE ORGANIZATION

From the earliest days of the Industrial Revolution, far-sighted and humane men like Robert Owen and the Cadbury Brothers have devoted much time and energy searching for ways in which employees could participate more fully in the prosperity which they helped to create. In recent times stock options, share issues and profit sharing have been

131

among the financial incentives used by companies to try and create a sense of involvement in their employees, and to enable them to share in prosperity. Of these, stock options almost invariably apply only to executives, and will thus be discussed further in the next chapter.

Share Issues

A complaint made by economists is that a high percentage of a capitalist nation's wealth tends to be owned by too few people. A contrary complaint made by revolutionaries is that too many people in advanced countries own too many things – cars, houses, television sets and so forth. People with possessions are generally unwilling to risk them for the sake of nebulous promises, especially when ownership has been the result of much hard work.

There is little doubt that a widespread ownership of capital tends to produce political stability in a nation, but equally there are few ways in which the ordinary person can accumulate substantial wealth. In Britain, at least, there are really only two ways it can be done. Firstly, by inheritance, or secondly by starting a business, building it up, and then selling it for a capital sum. For the ordinary person neither of these is very likely, nor is a third method, which necessitates winning the football pools.

It must be admitted that substantial wealth (say £50,000 or more) is beyond the scope of nearly everyone who is working for a wage or salary, unless he has rich relations. In spite of this, everybody would like the opportunity of accumulating assets if they were able to do so. Whether they would sell the assets and spend the money is, of course, a moot point. Probably some would, but even so, on the evidence, the majority would retain them, welcoming the security they represent.

Manufacturing industry is the sole source of all the material benefits enjoyed by mankind. In the United Kingdom, $8\frac{1}{2}$ million people earn their living from it, but very few of these have any financial stake in it. This is surely undesirable, if for no other reason than that it perpetuates the distinction between those providing labour, and those providing capital, with all the friction that this entails. Another good reason is that employee ownership of shares results in a much greater awareness of the financial facts of business life. One still meets people who firmly believe that the directors of a company own all the shares, and that the company reserves, as quoted in the balance sheet, are kept in a large safe in the managing director's office. If these same people owned shares in their company, it would be strange if they did not become very well informed on matters relating to their business.

It is surprising how many industrialists would genuinely like their employees to share in the prosperity of their company. The only problem is to decide how this can best be done. An overall increase in earnings is always undesirable as this simply increases employment costs per unit of output, possibly at just the time when market forecasts indicate a recession in a few months' time. A Christmas special bonus is similarly questionable, since, if it is paid one year, employees expect it also to be paid the next year, irrespective of profitability. Thus, having thought of ninety-nine different solutions, each being discarded in turn for eminently sensible reasons, nothing eventually is done. Strangely enough, those who are most concerned about this are often the industrialists themselves, who feel that they ought to have been able to find a way to reward their employees without prejudicing the future of the company.

Share issue schemes for employees have been adopted by a number of companies in recent years, sometimes for political, but often for sociological and motivational reasons. In essence such schemes are designed to enable employees, subject to certain qualifications, to become shareholders, and thus to become part-proprietors of the business. As part-proprietors, there is the potential benefit to the company of having employees who are interested in it, are more likely to stay with it, and who will perhaps accept, more willingly than otherwise, any changes which are necessary for the prosperity of the business. On the other hand, it must be accepted that the incentive element of a share issue scheme is likely to be almost non-existent, if by incentive one means that which will encourage people to work harder. The incentive is altogether too remote to operate effectively. There is no apparent connection between a man's effort in, say, March of one year and his issue of shares perhaps in the following February. The most one can hope for is that, as a shareholder, the man will feel that he is achieving at least some additional return, over and above his normal remuneration, when the company is successful. As one employee shareholder stated in a recent interview, 'I am quite prepared to tighten my belt when the going is difficult. But I would strongly resent the company making good profits if it didn't recognize my contribution, however small and insignificant that may be.'

133

One of the best publicized employee share issue schemes of recent years is that operated by I.C.I. Ltd. Under this, employees receive a bonus related to their annual wage or salary, the amount depending on the gross dividend payable on the Ordinary and Preference stock of the company. After deduction of tax, the net bonus is invested in shares of the company, these being purchased at market price. The shares are held in trust on behalf of each employee until they reach a certain value, when they are transferred to him. As soon as they are registered in his name, the employee has all the rights of any shareholder, and can vote, receive dividends, or even sell the shares on the market if he so wishes. In the first few years of the scheme, 40 per cent of the beneficiaries did so wish.

Another form of share issue scheme is that developed by the Rugby Portland Cement Co. To initiate it, the company created an additional one million 'A' shares, these having special rights regarding dividends, but which did not become effective until the profits of the company rose appreciably above the level existing at the time the shares were created. Half the issue went to the shareholders, and half to the employees. An important feature of the R.P.C. scheme is that the shares have a Stock Exchange quotation. Employee shares can be sold at any time at par value, but at market value only at retirement or death.

It will be evident from this brief description of the scheme that, for a small initial outlay, those employees who have contributed to the development of the company can enjoy a considerable capital gain if profits develop as expected. In the words of the Chairman, Sir Halford Reddish, the underlying intention was 'to create conditions under which, by their own efforts, the employees could become substantial owners of capital, while maintaining in full the element of partnership with the ordinary shareholder'.

That British Rugby Portland Cement has had an outstanding profit record for many years is a matter of history. Could the share issue scheme perhaps have played a contributory part? Or would the profits have been just as good without it? One can never say with certainty. There is, however, something that can be said with certainty; the scheme recognizes that the company has a responsibility to its employees, providing as it does the financial security of what is virtually a non-contributory endowment policy which increases in value with the growth of the company. It is perhaps no coincidence that Sir Halford Reddish was a signatory to the Marlow Declaration.

Profit Sharing

Profit sharing may be defined as any arrangement whereby employees receive, in addition to their normal remuneration, a bonus based on the profits of the enterprise. Proverbially, the road to hell is paved with good intentions, and the intentions of those firms introducing profit sharing have undoubtedly been of the highest. In spite of this, over the last few years, out of 650 schemes introduced, 530 were subsequently discontinued. The great disadvantage about profit sharing is that it depends on profits. Regrettably, profits do not always exist, often for reasons entirely unconnected with the efforts of people in the organization.

The ideal condition for profit sharing is when profits slowly and regularly increase from year to year. Then everyone is happy, looking forward with keen anticipation to their yearly or half-yearly bonus. Should, however, the profits fail to materialize, and with them the bonus, then trouble begins. People suggest that the company ought to pay the bonus irrespective of the profits. (After all, many people may have booked their summer holidays in anticipation of the customary bonus.) Barrack room lawyers point out that the employees must have had a right to the extra money, otherwise the company would never have paid it. If it was their right, then it should be paid without further delay. So the arguments go on and on, until finally, possibly as a result of industrial action, the company surrenders, pays the bonus, and discontinues its philanthropic ideas.

Profits are notoriously sensitive to changes in the level of activity in a factory. This is a serious disadvantage to any bonus system, since a factory may have achieved, say, a 10 per cent increase in the productivity of materials, stock inventories and labour, and still show a reduction in absolute profit due to a shortage of orders. To suggest to the employees that they must accept a drop in bonus, although they have improved productivity by 10 per cent, is asking a great deal of human nature.

A method which has been devised to provide a bonus for improved efficiency, without the disadvantages experienced by employees under profit sharing, is based on Added Value. For any company, an important criterion of competitive ability is the output produced per £1 stg paid

135

in wages to the production operators. If we adopt Added Value as the measure of output, the wage cost per unit of output is thus equal to the Production Labour Cost divided by the Added Value, or Labour/ Added Value for short. Inverting this term, it is evident that the greater the Added Value created per £1 of Labour Cost, the greater the profitability of the company, other things being equal.

Group bonus schemes based on the relationship between Added Value and Production Labour have been used by a number of companies to encourage a sense of participation in employees. One company refers to their bonus as the 'Co-operative Dividend', and is very insistent that the bonus should be regarded entirely separately from the normal earnings, these consisting of an operational rate plus individual payment-by-results earnings.

There are several varieties of Added Value bonus, depending on the particular needs of the situation. For an example, we will examine a typical scheme introduced by a light engineering factory near Birmingham. The factory is engaged on batch production, and employs 200 people manufacturing pressings, mainly for the automobile industry. The preliminary action needed was to measure historically the Added Value created per £1 Production Labour cost. This review covered 18 months, and established a figure of £2·65 Added Value per £1 Labour. This was then taken as a reference, being allotted an index number of 100. To achieve stable wage costs per unit of output meant that this index should not fall below 100, and consequently the bonus scheme was designed to reflect this. The higher the ratio Added Value/ Labour, expressed as an index, the greater the ability of the company to pay, and hence the greater the bonus. Similarly, the lower the index, the lower the bonus.

The bonus is payable weekly. The index is calculated as a four-month moving average, the reason being to smooth out fluctuations which might occur over a shorter time span due to changes in stock levels.

The original bonus rates were as follows:

Index (2.65 = 100)	Bonus – £ per week
Less than 90	Nil
90–94	1·75
95–99	2·00
100–105	2·25
Over 105	2·50

The method of bonus calculated is given in Table 28.

TABLE 28: BONUS CALCULATION, MULTIPRESS LTD

	Jan.	Feb.	Mar.	Apr.	May	June
Added Value – £'000	42,000	45,000	44,000	47,000	46,000	44,000
Labour Cost – £'000	16,700	18,400	17,600	19,000	18,600	17,700
A.V.: Labour (monthly)	2·51	2·45	2·50	2.47	2·47	2·50
A.V.: Labour (4 m. ave.)	2·56	2·52	2·51	2·48	2·47	2·48
Index (2·65 = 100)	97	95	95	94	93	94
Bonus – £ per week	2·00	2·00	2·00	1·75	1·75	1·75

The management of Multipress made it clear to the shop stewards, right from the start of the scheme, that the company's objective, as far as production labour was concerned, was to stabilize the ratio Added Value : Labour. If they could produce twice the Added Value for the same number of people, there would be no objection whatsoever to paying everybody twice as much money. Management also made it clear that, if the total bonus available in any one month amounted to, say, £1,200 for the 150 people eligible under the scheme, management did not mind if this £1,200 was retained by the company, so that month by month a fund could be built up, credited to the employees. This fund would be available for a substantial Christmas bonus, sickness benefit, timekeeping bonus, or for any other purpose desired by the people involved. After considerable discussion, the majority decision was that the bonus should be distributed weekly, on a per capita basis. However, the fact that there was a choice in the matter was a definite point in favour of the scheme.

It may perhaps be of interest to comment that the management of Multipress never considered that their co-operative dividend provided much incentive to work harder. What it did do was to make people more aware of the need for productivity improvement, more amenable to the installation of high output, labour-saving presses, and more agreeable to females doing the work customarily done by men. (If females can produce as much Added Value per hour as men, but for a lower rate of pay, the Added Value : Labour would increase, as would the bonus.)

In a review of the scheme, three years after its inception, the managing director of Multipress commented that, in his opinion, the single most valuable feature had been the opportunity provided for communication. Previous attempts to run a Productivity Committee had failed,

137

because the works manager, after only a few meetings, ran out of ideas as to what he should communicate. Consequently, the productivity meetings degenerated into the usual tea, toilets, inadequate heating, too draughty, type of conference, and were discontinued by mutual consent.

With the introduction of the co-operative dividend, a monthly Dividend Meeting was convened, attended by three shop stewards, three shop floor representatives, the senior foreman and the works manager. At this meeting the dividend was announced. As may be expected, whatever the dividend, people wanted to know why it was not more. All sorts of questions were asked. Why had this order been taken at a low price? Why had the company started a night shift? What was the future policy regarding bought-out components? And so on and so forth. The meetings generally lasted for nearly two hours, but at the end those attending were certainly in a much better position to understand the policies of the company than they had been before. Of equal importance, the works manager was able to keep people informed on current matters of policy, in the sure knowledge that his words would be absorbed, due to their possible implication for future dividends.

The Multipress scheme is an example of a particular way of trying to involve people in the affairs of a company. Involvement does not have the same connotation as participation, which implies taking part in the decision-making processes of management. Management's job is to take decisions, and to work through the medium of others. It is no part of the job of a trade unionist to take part in the functions of management. Few of them would even want to, as it would restrict them in the pursuit of their proper duties, which relate to the improvement of conditions for their members.

Involvement means keeping people informed, making them feel that they matter, enabling them to ask questions, and sharing with them the benefits of prosperity. To these ends, profit sharing and similar schemes may well have a part to play, to a much greater extent in the future than in the past. It would, however, be naïve in the extreme to think that a greater sense of involvement, admirable though this may be, will ever eliminate the conflicts which occur in industry. It will certainly increase understanding and tolerance, but it will not result in an ending of industrial strife. This does not mean that more involvement of people

138

is unnecessary. What it does mean is that it should not be looked upon as a golden key to open the doors of perfect industrial relations. There is no such key.

Economically speaking there is no doubt that industrial harmony is an essential ingredient of profitable operation. Equally, profitable operation is in the long-term interests of all, in spite of cynical comments to the effect that in the long term we shall all be dead. Managers frequently devote much time, effort and genuine worry to the perennial problem of how best to ensure a fair reward for a fair day's work. If they are successful in finding an answer, they must remember that it may not necessarily be welcomed by the representatives of organized labour.

In the summer of 1970, a booklet was issued to officials of Britain's largest union, the Transport and General Workers Union. It was called *Plant Level Bargaining*, and contained many helpful hints for negotiators. In particular, it uttered a caution regarding the dangers of allowing employers to persuade union members that the interests of the company were the same as those of the employees. It further commented as follows on the subject of a fair day's work for a fair day's pay. 'This paternalistic concept is the very opposite of all the unions' objectives. There can never be anything fair about a master-servant relationship. All that any agreement ever achieves is a temporarily acceptable day's pay for a temporarily acceptable day's work.'

The motivation of human beings is a fascinating subject. What is right today may be wrong tomorrow. What works in one environment may be a failure in another. Every manager must achieve results through other people. The more he knows about them, of their likes and dislikes, suspicions and aspirations, the more likely he is to be successful, and with his success to benefit the entire organization.

Chapter 14

Prosperity and the Executive

It has been estimated that there are 350,000 managers in U.K. manu-facturing industry, amounting to about 4 per cent of the total manu-facturing labour force. On the abilities and expertise of this compara-tively small number depends the prosperity of many people.

Henri Fayol, one of the great pioneers of scientific management, and a contemporary of F. W. Taylor and Mary Parker Follett, suggested in his writings that managerial activities could be classified under the five headings of Planning, Organizing, Commanding, Co-ordinating and Controlling. Some theorists have a regrettable tendency to confuse cause and effect, but this never applied to Fayol, perhaps because he practised what he preached, being the successful managing director of a French mining company. He was constantly aware that the object of management is to produce a stated result, as is instanced by his defini-tion of control. 'Control,' he said, 'is seeing that everything occurs in conformity with established rule and expressed command.'

Management is concerned with the organization of resources. Above all, it is concerned with people, with defining objectives, and ensuring that these objectives are achieved. The effective manager – that is, the manager who can produce results – is one of the most valuable assets a company can possess. The ineffective manager is of little value, and should be rendered harmless by transfer to a functional duty, or, in extreme cases, asked to find another job. The most difficult case to deal with is that of the mediocrity, the man who carries out his duties con-scientiously, and to the best of his ability, giving no positive cause for dissatisfaction but somehow never revealing any real originality or strength of character. This is the man who always seems to do his best, works hard, but never achieves anything in particular. He may well be a useful member of the company at the lower levels, where reliability and loyalty may compensate for lack of initiative. At the higher levels, which he sometimes reaches as a result of his stolid virtues, he is likely to be a drag on the dynamism of the organization.

A business cannot afford mediocrity at the higher levels. Arjay Miller, a former President of Ford Motor, and currently Dean of the Stanford University Graduate School of Business, once said that good management is industry's scarcest resource. In his own words, 'The scarcity of management talent is a major bottleneck to getting things done.' His comments have been echoed by many leading industrialists, as well as by company analysts investigating the relationship between management ability and profitability.

In any company, large or small, the effectiveness of the organization depends, almost entirely, on a comparatively small number of key executives. To illustrate this, a company employing 700 people, with an annual turnover of £3,500,000, might typically have four full-time directors, including the chief executive. In addition there could be perhaps ten senior executives, the first three layers of the organization chart thus appearing as follows:

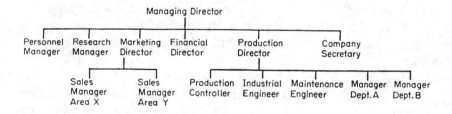

In total, the company payroll might be subdivided thus:

Directors	4
Executives	10
Other managers	12
Staff employees	144
Hourly paid	530
Total	700

In this typical company, it is probable that 90 per cent of the results achieved would emanate from the experience, judgment, initiative and

141

ability of not more than sixteen or so senior people – that is, less than $2\frac{1}{2}$ per cent of the total employees. No doubt the remaining six hundred and eighty-four would all be hard working, dedicated and loyal, but nevertheless, by the very nature of things, they could not possibly do more than marginally influence events. The decisions, actions and innovations on which the future of the company depended would be taken by the few and not by the many.

One of the most valuable characteristics which a senior executive can hope to find in a subordinate is the ability, and the willingness, to take decisions. Unfortunately, many subordinates, though perfectly able to take decisions, are unwilling to do so, since their careers might be adversely affected if they were proved wrong. Few executives are able to accumulate capital out of their earnings, and thus to provide themselves with a financial cushion in the event of losing their job, so there is a tendency for them to avoid risks. Taking decisions, especially major ones, involves a considerable element of risk, hence the temptation to opt out. One way of doing so is to convene a committee, and make sure that any decision is a joint one, which cannot be attributed to a particular individual. This is a solution which is not recommended in the interests of effective decision making, however attractive it may be to the individual who wishes to play safe. (On a not dissimilar subject, an inquiry of the Rumanian Institute for Economic Research in 1967 revealed that managers considered that $7\frac{1}{2}$ hours of their working day were concerned with inessentials; so much information had to be submitted to respective planning offices – to be on the safe side – that only a fifth of available time tended to be used; an annual plan might take up to six months to be handed down to the implementers; and so on.)

In his autobiography, *Slide Rule*, Nevil Shute recounts his experiences during the war, when he was seconded to the Admiralty. Nevil Shute, apart from being a best-selling author and a fine engineer, was also an acute observer of the daily scene. In a very short time he came to the conclusion that he was able to tell which Admiralty Civil Servants had private incomes, and which had not. The former were prepared to bypass procedures, cut red tape, and make decisions. The latter conformed, operated through established channels, and seldom made a decision on their own initiative. The former achieved results. The latter did not. After reading *Slide Rule* one is tempted to muse as to the fate of Britain had it not been for men of private means!

142

Ever since 1886, when output per man in the U.S.A. first exceeded that in Britain, working parties have crossed the Atlantic from east to west to investigate the reasons for the superior productivity of the American worker. There are, of course, many reasons why their productivity should be better, such as the size of the market, the natural mineral resources, the abundance of cheap power, and so forth. Nevertheless, discounting these, the working parties reported almost unanimously that a major factor was the high quality of American management. They commented that American managers are more cost conscious, more willing to delegate, and better trained than their British counterparts. (The Harvard Business School was founded in 1908. It was nearly fifty years later that the London and Manchester Schools were founded.) They commented that Americans are more dedicated to the profit motive, and show greater readiness to innovate. They sometimes mentioned that the vast majority of American managers participate in stock option schemes, and are eligible for profit-sharing bonuses if their company is prosperous.

Management Education

In recent years so much has been written regarding the need for more and more management education that one is hesitant to suggest that logic may have been diverted by emotion. Obviously, executives who are well versed in modern managerial techniques *ought* to be more capable than their untrained counterparts. Equally, the country with many well-established Business Schools *ought* to have a better administered and more competitive industry than the country with none. What is perhaps alarming is that so many people confuse 'ought to' with 'will be'. The danger lies in the too ready acceptance that better and better training will inevitably result in better and better managers. America has many highly trained managers, and a high level of productivity, but it would be naïve therefore to assume that the former is the sole cause of the latter. Without doubt, training has a part to play, but the exact extent must be a matter for debate. After all, German industry is highly dynamic and highly successful, yet their academic facilities for management education are quite rudimentary.

Until it is possible to equate training programmes with results achieved – and research to date indicates that it will be some time in the future before this can be done – the need for management training

143

must remain largely an act of faith. It is not wrong that this should be so, apart from the inherent difficulty of persuading the doubtful, who may demand positive proof before accepting that there is a need.

Job Definition

Training is only one stage in the improvement of management standards, its purpose being to provide job expertise. Another stage is ensuring that individuals know what they have to do, and the results they are expected to achieve. Numerous instances could be quoted of companies who have failed to define what they require of their staff. One chief executive stated, 'My people know perfectly well what they have to do. They are well paid for doing it.' Later, he admitted that the directors had never actually explained company strategy and tactics to the senior executives. Later still, he admitted that the directors themselves had never been briefed on company strategy. Finally, he confessed that, while personally quite clear on company policy, he had never communicated it to anyone else, relying on common sense to provide an understanding of the task.

The need for job definition, allocation of responsibilities – and responsibility is the best form of management development – performance appraisal, and reward for a job well done, is inherent in the philosophy of Management by Objectives. John Humble, whose original work in this area of management resulted in the award of the British Institute of Management Burnham Medal in 1966, has frequently stressed that it is not enough simply to agree what a man must do; one must also define what he must achieve. It is not enough merely for him to analyse a problem; he must also produce an action plan to solve it.

Executive Remuneration

Most American managers have a vested interest in their company, and in the market standing of its shares. The converse is true in Britain. Indeed, as was pointed out in an article* in *Management Today*, which surveyed the board-rooms of 200 top companies, shareholders should be very disturbed at the realization that most directors' personal fortunes are hardly affected by movements in their company's share price. Perhaps they should also be disturbed that American methods of

* September 1970.

144

remunerating executives are not more widely practised in the U.K., since it is quite possible, and even probable, that part of the dynamism of U.S. industry is the outcome of paying its executives by results.

In any discussion of executive remuneration, it is first necessary to consider whether the salaries paid by a given firm are approximately correct. There are several ways of checking this, as for example:

1. By monitoring job advertisements in the national papers and trade journals. The problem here is that advertised salaries are aimed at attracting high-grade applicants, and are thus likely to be 10–15 per cent above the average rate for the job. In addition, it is difficult to know the exact duties and responsibilities involved, since most advertising texts are not specific in this matter.
2. By participating in surveys, or by subscribing to publications giving details of executive salaries. This is a useful method, and one which provides a reasonable assessment of current rates. A disadvantage is that surveys often reveal a considerable spread about the median, due to factors which are not readily evident to the reader.
3. By discussing salary levels with senior executives in other companies, either through personal acquaintance, or as a result of contacts gained through membership of a professional body, such as the Institution of Works Managers.

Two other indicators may be mentioned. Firstly, a company may have difficulty in recruiting the necessary calibre of staff. Secondly, it may experience a high rate of managerial turnover. Either of these may be the result of uncompetitive rates, though they may also be due to an unsatisfactory company image, or restricted promotion prospects.

As previously stated, the vast majority of British companies do not operate schemes for paying their executives by results. Nor do they generally favour schemes intended to provide a financial stake in the company, with all that such a stake implies in furthering an interest in the company's market standing. One reason why they do not may be due to an understandable reluctance to pay a bonus which does not necessarily depend directly on the contribution of a given individual. How can one relate the efforts of, say, the production director to the profits of the company? Did not the managing director use the increased production as a reason to reduce prices to try and increase market share, thus adversely affecting profits in the short term? What about the

145

one-week strike which cost the firm £100,000? Would it have lasted twice as long if it had not been for the negotiating genius of the personnel manager? Or would it never have happened at all if he had not been so obtuse?

There are a number of valid reasons why it is apparently unfair to pay bonuses to executives. An alternative way of looking at it is to say that there are also a number of valid reasons why it is apparently unfair to shareholders not to pay such bonuses. If these bonuses were to result in more effective management, the lack of them certainly would be considered unfair. Similar considerations could apply to the encouragement of share ownership and stock option schemes, yet rarely does one encounter the attitude that a financially secure executive is more likely to take honest decisions than his insecure colleagues. On the contrary, the attitude to capital-based remuneration schemes, such as stock options, appears to be that they are vaguely immoral, and must be discouraged by adverse propaganda and swingeing taxation. What never seems to be considered is that payment by results and financial security might conceivably provide just the right combination for managerial motivation.

Executive Bonus Schemes

The rationale of a bonus is that it provides an individual with an incentive to achieve certain goals. There are, of course, many complications in equating executive effort to results, but in spite of these a number of companies are firmly convinced of the value of payment-by-results bonuses for their key executives. In terms of numbers these key executives may represent less than 3 per cent of the total employed; in terms of influence they can make or break the business.

When evaluating bonus schemes, certain questions must always be asked. The three most important are:

1. Does the bonus represent a significant proportion of basic salary?
2. Can the man, by his personal efforts, directly affect his level of bonus?
3. Is the bonus dependent on the attainment of specific and measurable results?

To qualify as a sound scheme, the answers to the above must be in the affirmative. Subsidiary requirements are that the scheme must be considered fair and equitable by the participants, and that the level of bonus is not liable to fluctuate widely due to changes in product mix.

A bonus which yields less than 15 per cent of a man's basic salary is unlikely to provide a satisfactory incentive. Experience has shown that a figure of 20–25 per cent is necessary, and the cost of making payments of this magnitude is a telling reason for limiting them to key staff only.

The ability of a man directly to influence his rate of bonus is a very necessary feature of any payment by results scheme. With executives it is particularly difficult to ensure this, due to the mutually complementary nature of most high-level actions. This leads on to the question of results. Preferably, more than one criterion should be used for bonus determination. For example, the bonus of the production director might be based on achieving targets related to unit wage costs, delivery performance, and rejection levels. Each of these is of considerable importance, and their use as a measure of performance would serve three ends. Firstly, it would stress that the duties of the manager concerned involve more than simply meeting the output budget. Secondly, it would provide the possibility of earning bonus even if, for example, interruptions in material supply made it impossible to maintain the requisite delivery performance. Thirdly, it would emphasize particular factors which are the undoubted responsibility of the production director.

Having defined the targets in general terms, the next step is to decide the objective performance standards. These must obviously be capable of measurement, otherwise numerical values could not be applied, the whole exercise thus becoming a nonsense. Typical targets might be agreed as follows:

Bonus Factor	*Performance Standard*
Unit Wage Cost	To maintain wage costs per unit of output at the average level applying in the period January–June 1971. Target. £1 labour cost per £3·6 Added Value produced.
Delivery Performance	To achieve a delivery performance such that the majority of orders are delivered by the due date. Target. 90% of orders delivered on time.
Quality	To improve the quality of the product delivered to customers by 10% as compared with 1970 standards. Target. Returns from customers not to exceed 0·8% of invoiced sales.

Since three factors are to be considered when assessing performance, these must be rated in order of importance. Let us say that the total points to be awarded when all the targets are reached is 100, made up of 55 for wage cost control, 30 for delivery performance, and 15 for quality. Certain assumptions must now be made regarding the points to be awarded for performances greater or less than standard, and these are tabulated as shown in Table 29:

TABLE 29: PERFORMANCE AND POINTS RATING

Level of Achievement	BONUS POINTS		
%	Unit Wage Cost	Delivery Performance	Quality
Less than 70	Nil	Nil	Nil
70–79	11	6	3
80–89	30	18	9
90–94	47	25	13
95–99	51	28	14
100–104	55	30	15
105–109	60	32	15

The final stage is to decide the level of bonus, and the fluctuation against performance, and to equate points to bonus. Possibly the chief executive might decide that 100 points should be worth 20 per cent of the production director's basic salary, and that the bonus should be paid every three months. The bonus calculation would then be as follows, assuming certain hypothetical levels of achievement:

TABLE 30: BONUS CALCULATIONS

Period	Wage Cost % – Points		Delivery % – Points		Quality % – Points		Total Points	% Bonus
July–September	98	51	96	28	101	15	94	18·8
October–December	96	51	90	25	98	14	90	18·0
January–March	94	47	92	25	86	9	81	16·2
April–June	92	47	87	18	82	9	74	14·8

Annual Salary – £6,000 (£1,500 per quarter)
Bonus Payable:

July–September	£282 ($\frac{1}{4}$ of 6,000 × 18·8%)
October–December	£270
January–March	£242
April–June	£222

It will be evident that the total bonus for the year amounts to £1,016. The overall cost to the company of paying bonus to perhaps thirty key executives would be of the order of £25,000. From a consideration of the production director's salary, the company would probably have a turnover of some £15 million, employing 3,000 people, and paying £3½ million in wages and salaries. Thus, in perspective, the total bonuses would represent 0·71 per cent of payroll costs.

The foregoing example is indicative of the sequences involved in preparing a payment-by-results scheme for executives. In practice, such schemes require a great deal of thought, and analysis of corporate and individual objectives. They all have the same purpose – to improve the effectiveness of managers.

Stock Options

A stock option may be defined as a legal right to purchase shares in a company, at a specified price and specified dates.

When considering the implications of various types of remuneration, it is often useful to quote an actual example. In this instance we will describe the case of an executive in a leading American chemical company. In 1967 this executive was appointed vice president of one of the company's operating divisions. Among the incentives awarded at the time of his promotion were cash bonuses of up to $15,000 per year – awarded in proportion to company profitability – and the right to purchase stock, in blocks of 1,000 shares per year, over a five-year period. The option price was $35 per share.

At the end of 1968 the share price was 42, and he purchased his first allocation for $35,000. One year later the price had risen to 53, and he purchased the second block for a further $35,000. By this time he was showing a surplus of $36,000, and seven months later, sensing national economic decline, he sold all the stock and realized a substantial profit.

The above is typical of the happy ending which all recipients of stock options hope to achieve. Unfortunately, disaster can sometimes strike, as nearly happened to a colleague of the vice president mentioned above. This man had accumulated 2,000 shares by 1970, for which he had paid $70,000. To finance the purchase, he had borrowed $60,000 from the bank, against the security of the shares, as well as using $10,000 of his own savings. Out of loyalty to the company, and because he had faith in its future, he decided not to sell his shares, but by August 1970 the market value had reduced to 32, and the bank was becoming anxious

149

lest its loan should not be adequately covered. Fortunately this was the lowest point reached, and by the end of the year the stock had recovered to 36. Nevertheless, the executive concerned was close to losing a great deal of money through no fault of his own, which caused him to become very disillusioned about the virtues of stock options.

Stock option schemes have never been adopted by more than a few companies in Britain. This lack of interest can be attributed to several factors, such as the inability of the individual to influence share prices, the effect on such prices of the vagaries of the stock market, and the suspicion that stock options provide no real incentive towards more effective management. As regards the last factor, it is certainly true that, since the 1965 Finance Act, stock options have had little attraction. This Act stipulated that consequential capital gains should be taxed as income in the year in which the option was exercised, thus virtually destroying any financial benefit for the already highly taxed company executive.

In the U.S.A., stock options have had considerable vogue for over twenty years. In 1968, two out of every three companies quoted on the New York Stock Exchange operated some form of option arrangement. At Board level, 90 per cent of top American executives participated in such schemes, most of them receiving annual cash bonuses in addition. It must be admitted that American tax legislation used to be very favourable with respect to stock options, capital gains tax being levied only when the beneficiary sold his shares on the market. This situation changed appreciably with the tax reform law passed by Congress in 1969. Not only did this law substantially increase the rate of capital gains tax, but it also included a clause specifying that the benefits resulting from optioned stock should be treated as 'tax preference' income. As such, these benefits were subjected to a 10 per cent surtax – in addition to the increased tax on capital gains. As a result of this law one thing seems certain. Stock options will lose much of their attraction as a means of rewarding American executives.

The proponents of option schemes claim that they fulfil several purposes. They accent the need for profits, since it is a company's profit record which largely conditions stock market valuations. They encourage long service, and they provide a lure to assist company recruiters in their search for managerial talent. Any or all of these may be perfectly valid, but it must be remembered that there are several

150

counter arguments. Firstly, the individual in a large company is rarely able to influence share prices, whatever his efforts, and this is likely to result in a minimal incentive effect. Secondly, although there may be every encouragement for an executive to remain in his job so that he can exercise, or continue to exercise, his option rights, there are instances when, once he has done so, he has immediately resigned, joined another company, and started all over again. Thirdly, with current taxation rules, few people are likely to be greatly influenced in their choice of jobs by the promise of stock options.

Restricted Stock

Exercising his right to a stock option involves an individual in considerable risk. Not only does he have to produce a large sum of money to purchase his entitlement, but he is also liable to lose heavily if share prices should fall.

A less risky device for rewarding executives has been adopted by some companies, such as American Cyanamid, Uniroyal, and Dow Jones, by the issue of 'restricted stock'. Such stock may be granted either as a bonus, or as a purchase at very advantageous terms – say 50 per cent of market value. The stock is similar to conventional stock, with one important exception; it cannot be sold for a stated period of time, and frequently not until the holder retires. If he leaves the company prematurely then he forfeits any advantage, and must sell the stock at the price he paid for it.

Notional Stock

Some companies overcome the problem of dilution of shareholders' equity, inherent in any share issue scheme, by awarding notional shares to their key executives. Again the object is to improve performance through a sense of proprietary interest, the shares being awarded for long service, company profitability, or attainment of specified objectives.

Notional stock, often described as imaginary or phantom stock, qualifies for dividends in exactly the same way as real stock. If the company declares a dividend of 15 per cent on its ordinary stock, then the notional stockholders would also receive 15 per cent, payable as a bonus. In most cases notional stock is credited to the recipients at a

151

given market price, and may be 'sold' back if the price improves, the difference between the two prices being credited in the form of a cash bonus.

The Remuneration Package

Prior to the 1914–18 war the majority of British industry was in private hands, with only about 20 per cent of the companies having a stock exchange quotation. The managers of the private companies were often also the owners, and tended to be more interested in capital accumulation than in the income they received. In the 1920s and 1930s the position changed radically, and by 1970 a survey of 200 of Britain's top companies revealed that only one in seven of the directors had any family connection with the business.

During the half century or so during which businesses changed from being managed by owners to being managed by paid executives, methods of executive remuneration hardly changed at all. Bonuses were rare, and remuneration consisted of a salary, pension contributions and possibly a car. Many companies conformed to the principle of an annual salary survey, whereby each executive and manager was assessed in terms of age, experience and performance. Following the assessment, increases would be awarded, after due consideration had been given to changes in the cost of living during the previous year. If retail prices had risen by $3\frac{1}{2}$ per cent, then everyone would receive at least a $3\frac{1}{2}$ per cent increase. (Some companies recognized that, due to the incidence of taxation, a 6 per cent increase would be necessary to give a $3\frac{1}{2}$ per cent improvement in take-home pay for the average manager, but such companies were in the minority.) Above average people might receive a $5–7\frac{1}{2}$ per cent increase, and outstanding people a 10 per cent increase. While there was considerable acceptance of the theory that an executive's *rate* of salary increase is more important than his *absolute* salary, nevertheless salaries tended to conform more to the philosophy of a rate for age rather than of a rate for results achieved. This view was substantiated by a recent survey carried out on behalf of the Institution of Works Managers, in which a strong correlation was indicated between age and salary level. Indeed, the comment was made that it appeared that Works Managers were paid more simply for growing older!

In the 1960s considerable changes occurred in attitudes towards executive remuneration. There was an increasing recognition of the shortage of managerial talent, resulting in companies urgently reviewing their payment systems, not only to attract but also to retain men of consummate ability. One international corporation devised a remuneration package consisting of basic salary, stock options, restricted stock bonuses, life, health and termination of employment insurance contributions, top hat pension, expense account, and the right to use the company yacht for week-end or holiday cruising. This company was certainly not being philanthropic in providing such a range of rewards. Its successful managers could amass considerable wealth, but the unsuccessful soon learned the object of 'termination of employment' insurance.

In America, many companies are convinced of the efficacy of paying executives by results. In Britain, the disadvantages are generally considered to outweigh the advantages. The taxation system seems to have been designed specifically to discourage any scheme whereby results are rewarded by the opportunity for share ownership. On a wider front, such discouragement applies also to schemes aimed at employee participation. As an example of this, let us suppose that a company wanted all its employees to become part owners, and decided to increase the nominal capital so that it could make a gift of shares to each person. Firstly the shareholders would have to renounce their right to these bonus shares, for no consideration. Then they would be subjected to capital gains tax on the value of the shares they had renounced. Finally, the employees who received the shares would be assessed for tax, on the theory that the shares represented income in the year they were awarded.

Every company aspires to profitability, and seeks to ensure that it has effective executives. Such men are not easy to find. They must have many characteristics, including a knowledge of modern management techniques, and an ability to locate the really important areas of a company's activity. They must be able to innovate, to take decisions, and to achieve results.

Some men respond to the motivation of power, some to honours, and some to money. If a system of executive remuneration were devised which would increase the supply of capable men, their combined contributions could well revolutionize the productivity of industrial resources.

Chapter 15

Company Income and the Value Added Tax

It is generally recognized that the ability of a company to generate and sustain profitable growth depends, almost entirely, on the success it achieves in a relatively small number of key result areas. Studies in the United States have shown a remarkable similarity of views regarding the identity of these areas, the seven most important being:

> Market position
> Current profitability
> Employee motivation
> Management development
> Public responsibility
> Innovation
> Command over financial resources

The corporate objectives of many companies lay great emphasis on the results to be achieved in each of these key areas, and in particular on the need to innovate.

Long term survival is impossible without innovation. This is as true for the innovation of ideas as for the innovation of new products. An interesting example of the former, relevant in the present context, occurred in 1790, when plans were being prepared for the first census of the United States. At that time the States had a population of four million persons, mainly engaged in agriculture, and the Federal authorities were resolved to measure the output of the newly founded nation. Consequently, the Treasury decided to ask all enterprises to submit details of their value of sales during the census period, so that these could be totalled, and the output assessed. At this point, a Treasury official named Cox had a bright idea. Rather than companies submitting their value of sales, which would give an inflated estimate of national output, Cox decided that they should submit their value of sales *less* the value of everything they had bought. This residual value, or as we would call it, 'Added Value', could then be totalled, industry by industry, or product by product, to give the true output of the economy.

In the event, the 1790 census did not include data relating to industrial output. It was not until 1850 that a comprehensive set of statistics was collected, showing, among other interesting facts, that the output of the economy amounted to $308 per head! Nevertheless, the basic innovation of 1790 was incorporated in the 1850 census, and subsequently adopted by almost every major industrial country for the measurement of national output.

Added Value analysis has long been used by national statisticians, but it is only comparatively recently that it has been adopted by companies who have been dissatisfied with the limitations of the more conventional indicators of performance. 'Added Value' is not an esoteric term invented to confuse the uninitiated. It is simply a name given to identify the net income of a company, just as 'Contribution' is the name given to identify the residual obtained by deducting variable costs from sales value.

An important reason for adopting statistics based on Added Value is that this enables a company to define, absolutely clearly and unambiguously, what it is trying to achieve in all its actions – namely, to create an income. Initially, this requires an intense communication exercise, but, once the concept has been understood, the company can then proceed to prepare and quantify its key objectives. Having defined the plan, then an integrated management accounting system can be developed, covering the entire control function, and including costing, estimating, pricing, financial ratios, and budgetary control. In certain cases, Added Value can be used as the base measurement for productivity bonus schemes, although, as with all payment systems, extreme care must be taken to select the most appropriate application for a given set of circumstances.

We have seen, in preceding chapters, how Added Value can be applied as the basic measure of company income and output. There is yet another area where it is relevant, namely that of taxation.

A value-added tax, or VAT as it is generally known, was first introduced in France in the 1950s, and was subsequently adopted by the

155

Council of the E.E.C. in 1967 as a common system of tax among the member states of the economic community. By January 1970 all these states had incorporated VAT in their respective tax structures, as had certain other European countries such as Denmark.

VAT is a method of taxation whereby goods are taxed at each stage of production in proportion to the value added by the process of production. This Added Value is obtained by deducting, from the value of sales, the cost of all raw materials and other bought-out purchases. Expressed another way, Added Value is equal to the wage and salary costs, plus depreciation and all other fixed expenses, plus profit. Thus, in general terms, the more the workmanship applied to a product, the higher the Added Value, and the greater the liability to VAT.

VAT is a multi-stage tax, levied at each stage of production. Purchase Tax is a single-stage tax, levied when a sale is made to the final consumer, and paid by the consumer to the final vendor, who in turn remits the tax to the Inland Revenue. Turnover tax is a multi-stage tax, but it has the disadvantage that it involves taxing a tax, which is a bad fiscal principle.

VAT may be levied at a single rate, as in Denmark, or at differential rates, as in Germany and France. The advantage of a differential rate is that it enables favourable treatment to be given to, say, extractive industries, reasonable treatment to manufacturing industries, and penal treatment to service industries, should such variations be deemed necessary in the interests of the economy as a whole.

HOW VAT IS CALCULATED

The calculation of VAT liability is shown in the following example, where a primary producer A sells to a manufacturer B. B sells to a wholesaler C, and C to a retailer D. Finally, D sells to the consumer.

In the example it is assumed that a single rate of VAT at 10 per cent is levied at each stage.

It is evident from Table 31 that the tax payable at each stage is calculated by taking 10 per cent of the selling price (excluding VAT), and deducting from this the element of tax already paid by the previous supplier in the chain. This is, of course, the same as levying a 10 per cent tax on the difference between Selling Price and Purchase Price at each stage, both excluding VAT.

TABLE 31: CALCULATION OF VAT

	Company				
	A	B	C	D	Consumer
Purchase price (exc. VAT)	0	100	200	300	450
Purchase price (inc. VAT)	0	110	220	330	495
Selling price (exc. VAT)	100	200	300	450	
VAT @ 10%	10	20	30	45	
Selling price (inc. VAT)	110	220	330	495	
VAT liability	10	20	30	45	
VAT credit	Nil	10	20	30	
Net tax payable per stage	10	10	10	15	

Total cost to consumer 495
Total tax payable 45

Among the advantages claimed for VAT is that it can cover a very wide range of goods and services, thus providing a broad base for taxation. This is always a good thing to do, since the greater the number of items taxed, the less the rate of tax needed per item to produce a stated revenue, and hence the lower the distorting effect on the economy as a whole.

Another advantage claimed is that, since it is levied broadly in proportion to the wage and salary costs, plus profit, firms would have an incentive to increase labour productivity, and thus to reduce their tax liability. It is perfectly true that a company with higher conversion costs would include a higher element of tax in its selling price, as shown in Table 32. However, the difference is small, and not, by itself, likely to impair competitive ability.

A feature of VAT which is worth noting is that each company in the supplier/purchaser chain, with the exception of the final consumer, in effect makes an interest-free loan to the taxation authorities, of an amount equal to its tax liability. The duration of the loan is from the time the tax has been paid until the company receives payment from its customer. This feature of VAT could well provide a stimulus for firms to improve their system of credit control, so that they can reduce the capital required to finance VAT payments. Obviously the sooner the tax has to be paid after goods have been despatched, the greater the stimulus.

TABLE 32: EFFECT OF DIFFERING CONVERSION COSTS ON VAT

	Company		
	B	b	C
Purchase price (exc. VAT)	100	100	200 (B) or 180 (b)
Purchase price (inc. VAT)	110	110	220 (B) or 198 (b)
Selling price (exc. VAT)	200	180	
VAT @ 10%	20	18	
Selling price (inc. VAT)	220	198	
VAT liability	20	18	
VAT credit	10	10	
Tax payable	10	8	

HOW VAT IS COLLECTED

The liability of a company to VAT can be calculated in several different ways. The tax could be levied directly on the Added Value created, or on the value of Sales, with an offsetting credit on the value of purchases, or by two-part invoicing, showing tax as a separate item. Of these, the latter two have been extensively studied, and have been named the 'accounts' method and the 'invoice' method respectively.

The accounts method is reasonably simple. It will be evident from Table 31 that the tax due at each stage is calculated by adding 10 per cent, or 1/10th, to the selling price (excluding tax). Exactly the same result would be obtained by deducting 1/11th from the selling price (including tax). If we consider the transaction when B sells to C, it is easy for B to estimate his tax liability by deducing 1/11th, or 20, from the selling price (including tax) of 220. Similarly, B knows that A's liability must have been 1/11th of 110, or 10. Thus B can remit to the Inland Revenue the sum of 20–10, or 10, which is his net tax liability.

The accounts method is perfectly feasible if VAT were always levied at a single rate. As it happens, most countries operating a VAT system have several rates of tax, so that they can encourage or discourage different sectors of the economy as the need arises. Even if, like Denmark, they have only one rate, it is never safe to assume that differential rates will not be adopted at some time in the future, and for this reason it is sensible to standardize on a method of collection which permits this. This is doubtless the reason why the invoice method has been adopted by all European companies operating a VAT system.

The invoice method necessitates issuing two-part invoices against all sales made by a company. The first part shows the 'excluding tax' selling price, and the second part the tax due. Referring again to company B, B's sales to C and B's purchases from A would be invoiced as follows:

| B sells to C | Invoice price 200+20 tax |
| A sells to B | Invoice price 100+10 tax |

To ascertain the tax due, B adds up the tax component of all sales, and deducts the tax component of all purchases. The residual represents his tax liability. It obviously makes little difference if all B's suppliers are showing tax on their invoices at different rates, or if B is selling to different markets at different tax rates. The arithmetic involved is exactly the same.

COSTS OF COLLECTION

The main objections raised against a Value-Added Tax are the excessive costs of collection, and the extra work involved for firms. As regards the latter, firms paying the tax would incur a considerable extension of their book-keeping activities. A given company would have to record the tax element quoted on the invoices of its suppliers, and on its own invoices to customers. At stated intervals it would have to total the tax on all invoices received and issued, and substantiate these against the tax rates applicable to different transactions. On these two counts alone the extra work would be considerable. However, even if we accept that modern accounting techniques may be able to minimize these costs, the same cannot be said of collection costs.

Various estimates have been made of the number of people who would be required to operate a VAT system. The most authoritative is undoubtedly given in the NEDO* report, called *Value Added Tax*, which suggests that an extra 8,000 civil servants would be needed. If we assume that this number would represent a cost of £20 million per year, then it is readily apparent that Britain will be faced with a substantial increase in tax administration costs when she adopts VAT in 1973.

* H.M.S.O.

Many countries, including the United States, have investigated the merits of a tax on Value Added. As with all systems of taxation, the justification depends on a fine balance between costs of collection, public acceptability and political expediency, on the one hand, and revenue raised, on the other.

VAT has both advantages and disadvantages, but at least one can say this in its favour. It forces companies to examine the fundamental factors which affect tax liability. If, as a result, this leads to greater industrial efficiency, then VAT would fully be justified on this feature alone.

FURTHER READING

R. J. Ball   *Inflation and the Theory of Money*   Allen & Unwin 1964

J. Batty   *Standard Costing*   Macdonald & Evans 1966

A. J. Bergfeld, J. S. Earley & W. R. Knobloch   *Pricing for Profit and Growth*   Prentice Hall 1962

P. F. Drucker   *The Practice of Management*   Heinemann 1955

P. F. Drucker   *Managing for Results*   Heinemann 1964

F. Herzberg   *Work and the Nature of Man*   Staples Press 1968

J. Humble   *Management by Objectives in Action*   McGraw Hill 1970

Institute of Cost & Works Accountants   *Employee Remuneration & Incentives*   I.C.W.A. 1962

I.C.W.A.   *Cost & Management Accountancy for Students*   Heinemann 1968

J. Pen   *Modern Economics*   Pelican Books 1969

P.E.P.   *Thrusters and Sleepers*   Allen & Unwin 1965

J-J. Servan Schreiber   *The American Challenge*   Pelican Books 1969

Glossary

ABSORPTION COSTING
A costing method whereby all costs, both fixed and variable, are charged to cost centres or products, so that every item of cost is completely absorbed by that cost centre or product.

ADDED VALUE
The net income of a company. That sum of money which remains after the value of all bought-out raw materials and other purchases has been deducted from the value of sales. Also called *Value Added* or *Residual Value*.

BREAK-EVEN CHART
A graphic representation of the relation between total income and total costs for various levels of production and sales, indicating areas of profit and loss. (A.S.M.E.)

BUDGET
An organized statement of intended income and expenditure for a definite future period, usually a month or a year, made in order to assist in controlling expenditures, and to provide a criterion for judging performance during the period. (A.S.M.E.)

CAPITAL INTENSITY
A measure of the amount of capital used by a business, in order that it may produce goods or services. Generally measured in terms of capital per employee.

CONTRIBUTION
More fully, *Contribution to fixed expenses*. That sum of money which remains after all variable costs have been deducted from sales revenue.

FIXED COST
A cost which tends *not* to vary with changing levels of output.

161

GLOSSARY

MARGINAL COST

A cost which is equivalent to the cost of making one more of a product. The marginal cost is equal to the total variable costs of production.

PROFIT SHARING

An arrangement whereby employees receive, in addition to their normal remuneration, a bonus based on the profits of the enterprise.

STANDARD COST

The normal, expected cost of an operation, process or product, including labour, raw material, and overhead charges, computed on the basis of past performance costs, estimates, or work measurement. (A.S.M.E.)

STANDARD COSTING

A system of costing whereby standard costs are compared with actual costs, so that variances can be analysed, and their reasons assessed.

STOCK OPTION

A legal right to purchase shares in a company, at a specified price and on specified dates.

TOTAL COST

The total cost of a product, obtained by adding, to the variable costs of production, an apportionment of factory fixed costs.

VARIABLE COST

A cost which tends to vary with changing levels of output.

VARIANCE

The difference between actual and planned result, for any given variable.

VAT

Value Added Tax. A method of taxation whereby goods are taxed at each stage of production, in proportion to the value added by the process of production.

162

Index

163